Also by David Aaker

Owning Game-Changing Subcategories

Creating Signature Stories

Aaker on Branding: 20 Principles that Drive Success

Brand Relevance: Making Competitors Irrelevant

Three Threat to Brand Relevance (e-book)

Spanning Siloes: The New CMO Imperative

From Fargo to the World of Brands: My Story So Far 3rd Edition

*Brand Portfolio Strategy: Creating Relevance,
Differentiation, Energy, Leverage, and Clarity*

Brand Leadership (with Erich Joachimsthaler)

Building Strong Brands

Managing Brand Equity

*Strategic Marketing Management (11th edition)
(with Christine Moorman)*

Brand Equity and Advertising (edited with Alex Biel)

*Marketing Research 11 Edition
(with V. Kumar, Robert Leone, and George Day)*

Advertising Management 5th Edition
(with Rajeev Batra and John Myers)

Multivariate Analysis in Marketing
(2nd edition, editor)

Consumerism: Search for the Consumer Interest (4th Edition)
(edited with Georgy Day)

THE FUTURE OF PURPOSE-DRIVEN BRANDING

THE FUTURE OF PURPOSE-DRIVEN BRANDING

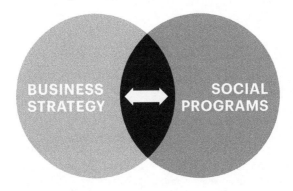

SIGNATURE PROGRAMS THAT
IMPACT & INSPIRE
BOTH BUSINESS AND SOCIETY

DAVID AAKER

NEW YORK

LONDON • NASHVILLE • MELBOURNE • VANCOUVER

THE FUTURE OF PURPOSE-DRIVEN BRANDING

Signature Programs that Impact & Inspire Both Business and Society

Published in New York, New York, by Morgan James Publishing. Morgan James is a trademark of Morgan James, LLC. www.MorganJamesPublishing.com

Proudly distributed by Ingram Publisher Services.

A **FREE** ebook edition is available for you
or a friend with the purchase of this print book.

_____

CLEARLY SIGN YOUR NAME ABOVE

Instructions to claim your free ebook edition:
1. Visit MorganJamesBOGO.com
2. Sign your name CLEARLY in the space above
3. Complete the form and submit a photo
   of this entire page
4. You or your friend can download the ebook
   to your preferred device

ISBN 9781631959882 paperback
ISBN 9781631959899 ebook
Library of Congress Control Number:
2022940012

Cover Concept by:
Stren Pipkin & Dani Kim

Cover Design by:
Christopher Kirk
www.GFSstudio.com

Interior Design by:
Chris Treccani
www.3dogcreative.net

Morgan James is a proud partner of Habitat for Humanity Peninsula
and Greater Williamsburg. Partners in building since 2006.

Get involved today! Visit MorganJamesPublishing.com/giving-back

To my wife Kay and
my daughters Jennifer, Jan, and Jolyn and their families.
They all support and inspire me every day.

Table of Contents

Chapter 1

THE FUTURE OF PURPOSE-DRIVEN BRANDING—THREE STRATEGIC THRUSTS

What we want for work is to be a valued member of a winning team on an inspiring mission.

Graham Weston, Entrepreneur

These are remarkable times for business organizations. It is a time of opportunity, even a time for dramatic change. It is not a time to stand still and drift toward irrelevance.

The new purpose-driven revolution is leading firms beyond a focus on growing sales, profits, and shareholder return to having a business purpose that does more. One that is meaningful, admired, and worthy of respect. One that engenders pride from employees, customers, partners, and other stakeholders. One that inspires people and firms to take on challenging tasks and goals.

There is a legend that Sir Christopher Wren, the architect of St. Paul's Cathedral in London, stopped one morning to ask three different laborers on the construction site, all engaged in the same task, what they were doing. He got three different answers. The first said, "I am cutting this stone." The second answered, "I am earning three shillings, sixpence, a day." The third man

1

straightened up, squared his shoulders and, still holding his mallet and chisel, replied. "I am helping Sir Christopher Wren build this great cathedral." People want to be building cathedrals and be associated with businesses that are doing just that.

An organization can have a purpose that goes beyond financials that does not involve addressing societal challenges. A purpose can, for example, be based on "creating insanely great products" or "offering the industry's best service." Or it can refocus from a product or service into what a product or service does. For instance, instead of trucking, we are the "lifeblood of communities" or instead of making cars, we "enable travel." These routes to a purpose can engender inspiration and, in general, elevate the opinion of a business and its brand for all its stakeholders. We here suggest that firms need to augment that perspective, to do more.

Addressing Societal Challenges

It is argued in this book that the "future of purpose-driven branding" will include addressing societal challenges with impactful programs. Sitting on the sidelines in the face of the problems and issues facing society is no longer a good option. Making great products is no longer enough to provide inspiration to a segment of employees and other stakeholders. It is now time to make sure that a business purpose or an accompanied social purpose includes addressing the serious problems, needs, and issues facing society. It is the road to being relevant in the purpose-driven era.

There are several forces that support the elevation of societal efforts for a business or firm that will be described in Chapter 4, In brief they are:

- **The stakeholder paradigm is winning.** In the battle with the "role of business is to increase shareholder wealth" business model, the good guys are winning. There are many indicators. One is the 2019 decision by the Business Round Table representing the CEOs of America's leading companies to adopt a new purpose that explicitly states that firms need to deliver value to all of the stakeholders and have a commitment to protect the environment. That means that a serious headwind to those espousing an aggressive social effort is now a soft breeze.

- **The seriousness and visibility of societal challenges.** There are enormous challenges facing society throughout the world, including climate change and inequality, that are increasingly visible and threatening. Many, especially the millennials, now believe that the threats are real and capable of dramatically affecting the quality of life and also a firm's long-term strategy and performance.

- **Businesses with resources, insights, and agility can contribute.** Firms need to be part of the solution because they are needed, they have the resources and agility to contribute, and for some issues such as obesity and inequality they have been part of the problem. Governments with political gridlock, resource limitations, and an inability to be agile and experimental, cannot do it all.

- **Employees and other stakeholders demand it.** In part, because of these three forces, many employees, particularly the younger generations, are uncomfortable in organizations that are not committed to authentic efforts to address societal challenges. They make join/leave decision based on the social purpose. Other stakeholders such as customers, suppliers, and investors are also on board. To be relevant to many stakeholders, a social purpose and programs are needed.

- **Business brands need the energy and image lift social programs provide.** A creditable set of social programs that address problems facing society have an unique ability to enhance a business brand. To get such a lift, the social programs need to stand out from the sea of sameness and represent distinctive societal leadership with authentic programs that have a "talked about" impact on societal challenges. The value of this business brand lift is particularly high when the business is bland or mature with few other ways to create interest.

A NOTE ON TERMINOLOGY

It is argued in this book, that the "future of purpose-driven branding" will include addressing challenges facing society such as environmental threats and inequality. We will describe these challenges as societal or social challenges where societal or social means that the challenges are relevant to or related to society in general and the welfare of human beings as members of society. We refer to responsive programs as social or societal programs or efforts where again social or societal means that the programs will address society's problems, needs, and issues. So the following have virtually the same meaning:

- Social or societal challenges/programs/efforts
- Challenges/programs/efforts that impact society

There are alternatives to the use of social or societal challenges/programs/efforts, namely "sustainable," "CSR" (corporate social responsibility) and "ESG" (environmental, social, governance). The terms "social" or "societal" or "society" are used here partially because the other terms, although playing a role in the discussion, have associations that are not helpful. The sustainable term, which can be traced to the 1980s, is often restricted to environmental programs and the CSR label, that appeared in the 1950s, is associated with dated ideas and programs.

The ESG concept was developed in 2005 by the finance community to guide investors who wanted a portfolio to include firms doing social good and avoiding social bad. This effort was supported by competing efforts by various organizations to measure the ESG performance of firms usually containing hundreds of dimensions, most of which are not relevant to a given firm. These ESG measuring services have sometimes struggled to show that they are measuring what they purport to measure. Additionally, because of all the dimensions covered, they do not focus on the impact made by programs that address major societal challenges. Nor do they measure the ESG performance of business units within a firm which for this book is often the more appropriate level of analysis.

Any organization that is now using and is comfortable with one of these three terms is not wrong and should feel free to use them when describing a society challenge, a social program, or societal efforts. It is not a label competition, it is the content behind the label that counts.

Purpose vs. Mission. A purpose or mission are two routes toward a high-level message about the essence of a firm or business that reflects its ambition to go beyond growing sales and profits to something far more motivating. The purpose or mission is usually a single sentence that is punchy, clear, and memorable and often is elaborated to provide detail and interpretation. It should inspire, guide, feel authentic and credible, and have a worthy goal.

Creating a purpose statement starts by asking the "Why?" question. Why does this business exist? Why do employees come to work? The mission statement is motivated more by the "What?" question. What is the task to which the organization is committed?

It is possible to have both a purpose and mission, but in most cases, they gravitate to a single thought that often incorporates both questions. The mission for Lego, for example, to "inspire and develop the builders of tomorrow," addresses both questions and suggests social programs as well. Here we use the two labels interchangeably to be relevant to firms that have adopted one but not the other, and to avoid distracting categorization issues.

A Lot of Upside Remains

Although there has been a lot of momentum building in the past decades toward a purpose-driven future involving societal efforts, the response needs to be greater and better. Even those firms that have the appropriate purpose or mission, the culture, and the programs in place, have work to do. There is an ongoing challenge in creating programs that impact society, in communicating them effectively to different stakeholders, in building and managing the many involved brands, and in scaling what is working. As the challenges persist and evolve, even these firms are far from reaching their potential.

There are also many firms that have either not gotten the word or have simply given lip service and not made an effort that is effective or even serious. There is still a distance to go to get these firms and their leaders on board. They need to find the motivation, the resources, and the right culture. Relying on ad hoc grants and volunteering is not enough to make a difference and it's not enough to affect the organization. These firms need to join the game and for some it will mean a major transformation of its purpose, culture, strategies, structure, and people.

Toward Social Program Leadership

The "future of purpose-driven branding" thus includes robust efforts to address societal challenges such as climate change, resource conservation, inequality, and improving health and well-being. That is not only the right and responsible course, but it should be the strategic choice as well. Survival in any marketplace involves becoming and staying **relevant** to employees and other stakeholders and a path to winning is to go beyond relevance to be a **social program leader.**

Real social program leadership means a commitment to create programs that inspire, are credible, and have a "make a difference" impact. It involves recognizing and analyzing society problems and issues with depth and insight, creating or finding programs that work, and then executing them with competence and passion. Inspiration is an important target. There should be social programs that get beyond being impressive. It should merit a "Wow!" reaction that breaks out of the sameness. And it should be branded.

There is a big payout for those that get it right. In addition to feeling good about the social good that is being done, those that claim a social program leadership position will enjoy a competitive advantage. Those that miss or stumble with their social effort will lose in the branding space and in the marketplace as well.

What is the future of purpose-driven branding? We can see three strategic thrusts or action plans, shown in Figure 1-1, that will represent the future for firms that strive to move beyond being relevant to being in a leadership position in the purpose-driven age.

- Attack society challenges with signature social programs
- Integrate the signature social program into a business
- Build inspiring, credible signature social brands

These will be examined in the course of the book after some context has been set in Part I in the form of two case studies and an overview of the forces diving the momentum toward social purpose enabled strategies. Parts II, III, and IV in turn introduce and analyze each of these strategic thrusts. In this chapter, a brief description of each will be presented to provide an overview of the challenge of winning in the purpose-driven age. It will conclude with an examination of the critical role of branding and a roadmap of the book.

Figure 1-1

SUCCESS IN THE PURPOSE-DRIVEN ERA

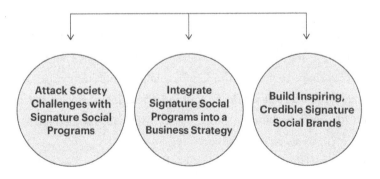

Success in the Purpose-Driven Era

- Attack Society Challenges with Signature Social Programs
- Integrate Signature Social Programs into a Business Strategy
- Build Inspiring, Credible Signature Social Brands

The Future—Attack Society Challenges with Signature Social Programs

The "future of purpose-driven branding" includes robust efforts to address societal challenges such as climate change, resource conservation, inequality, and improving health and well-being. That is not only the right and responsible course, but it should be the strategic choice as well. Survival in any marketplace involves becoming and staying **relevant** to employees and other stakeholders and a path to winning means going beyond relevance to be a **social program leader**.

Real leadership means a commitment to create social programs that are respected, admired, credible, and have a "make a difference" impact that inspire and even stimulate a "Wow!" reaction. And they are branded. We call these programs signature social programs.

Having signature status means that a program:

- Will address a meaningful societal challenge that touches people, that feels real emotionally.
- Is credible, impactful, and committed. It will make a difference.
- Will lift the energy and image of a business brand.
- Will build a visible, inspiring brand with the help of business partners that will guide the program and lead its communication task.
- Can be an internal program or an external nonprofit partner.

Why a signature social program? For perspective, much of the social effort of a firm or business usually consists of grants and volunteering which are and feel fragmented, without direction, having little aggregate impact, very similar to the effort by other firms, and unbranded. There is often an environmental component, perhaps to reduce the CO_2 emission and energy use, which does have a focus and goals but is also unbranded, looks like that of other firms, and can sound like puffery. Finding proof points and communicating them is thus often from formidable to impossible.

Signature social programs are needed because they are more likely to represent a real impact. They will have been set up to succeed by addressing a real need with a well-thought out and managed program that has focus. The programs will represent a long-term commitment which leads to improving features and operations and thus more impact. Their brand will provide direction and inspiration which is a large part of the success journey

They also provide value because a branded, focused program can communicate much easier and more effectively than a loose assortment of grants, volunteer activities and energy goals. Communication is a role that a brand plays. The signature program brand will have an uniqueness and impact story to tell about the program and about the business that it represents.

Communicating the efforts of a firm to address society challenges will only become increasingly critical. It is critical to create buy-in, engagement, and a sense of purpose among the firm stakeholders, particularly employees and customers or clients. It is critical to provide energy and inspiration to the program externally and internally. It is critical to enhance business partners. It is critical to gain visibility, to stand out from the perceived sameness around societal efforts of other firms.

The signature social programs can be an internal branded program such as Chick-fil-A's Shared Table program that provided over 10 million meals during its first decade after its founding in 2012 by a Tennessee operator. Or it can be an external partner. Costco, for example, has a "visionary partner" status for Feeding America supporting a program to supply to those in need food that otherwise would go to waste.

There is a big payout for those that get it right. In addition to feeling good about the social good that is being done, those that claim a social program leadership position will enjoy a competitive advantage. Those that miss or stumble with their social effort will lose in the branding space and in the marketplace as well.

Chapter 6 has more.

Getting a signature social program right is more likely if it is supported by an organizational purpose or mission and culture and if the right program is selected at the outset.

Create a Purpose or Mission & Culture that Nurture Social Programs

Creating or finding signature social programs and integrating them into a business starts by adjusting the DNA of the firm or business so that addressing societal problems and issues is an active part of the firm. It is just "what we do."

That means that proposals for a new or enhanced program does not have to answer the "why" question, only the efficacy standard. It means that societal challenges and programs become part of the strategy conversation and resourcing decisions. A purpose or mission (a mission can play the same role as the purpose—see the terminology insert for an explanation) and a strong culture are needed to help establish and reinforce this DNA.

A **purpose** or **mission** can be relevant for both a business strategy and its societal efforts. CVS Health is about "Helping people on the path to better health," and Foot Locker strives to "inspire and empower youth culture." When a business has a business strategy and brand position based on having an offering that is "green" or "healthy," the purpose or mission will then, of course, include a social component.

It is more common, however, to have a social purpose or mission separate from the business purpose or mission which, for some, can get diluted or distorted when an effort is made to include addressing societal challenges. When unconstrained, both can be free to be more complete, more forceful, and more credible. That does not mean that the social purpose or mission has less priority or a lesser role in the culture of the firm. Nor does it mean that they occupy different silos that are unconnected. They should be complementary, even overlapping, and have staffs and programs that interact and even intertwine.

One approach is to have multiple purpose or mission statements, one of which enables social programs. Caterpillar, for example, has four mission statements that inform strategies and decisions—to provide the best customer value, to develop and reward people, to grow, and a fourth reflecting a dedication *"to improving the quality of life while sustaining the quality of our earth. We encourage social responsibility."*

Some firms put their social purpose or mission in a companion foundation organization. Others can attach it to the corporate brand. Unilever has a mission to "aim to make sustainable living commonplace with high-performing brands that are a force for good, taking action for a more sustainable and equitable world." Each of the over 100 Unilever business units can own that social mission which gives them latitude when creating a purpose or mission for their business whether to include an explicit societal dimension.

The **organizational culture**, the "how we do things here" standard, brings the purpose or mission to life inside the firm. It is the beliefs, values, priorities, behavior, and management styles that determine how the organization and its employees view and act on issues and options that come before them. In a strong culture, there is an organizational force that provides people with an instinct as to what is comfortable and feels right. Whether it is a decision to commit to a nonprofit relationship, to start a social program, or to participate in an interest community around a societal issue, it makes a difference if it fits with the culture. To understand the culture, look to what decisions and behavior are valued, what actions or activities precipitate discomfort, and what programs are celebrated.

The challenge is to make sure that the culture of the firm permits or even celebrates the social effort. To do so, the commitment to the effort by the CEO and other leaders is critical, but not enough. Most of the organization should believe that a pressing, societal need is being addressed with credible signature programs that inspire, and numerous employees should be actively involved as volunteers or program leaders. In that case, the effort will become part of the culture and the wind will be at its back.

Chapter 5 elaborates.

Find or Develop Signature Programs that Deliver Social Impact

Businesses need to start by finding, creating, or reenergizing signature social programs. Ideas can come from a wide array of sources. The goal is to emerge with programs than touch a nerve, inspire, are credible, fit your business, and impact a real need.

One place to start is with your own assets, and offerings. How can you leverage what you have and what you do to support a social program? We shall see in Chapter 3, for example, Salesforce leveraging its software to aid nonprofits and firms that want to take sustainability efforts to a more professional level. The result is a set of programs that are credible, impactful, and ownable. They benefit from the software advances made in adjacent commercial products and from the perceived commitment of the firm's brand to these programs.

But a business is not restricted to using its own assets or having a natural fit. Some firms are not in a business with leverageable assets or with a natural connection from a social program to their business. They are then free to find a program that is needed and create a connection that reflects a passion, in-depth knowledge, and long-term commitment. In the next chapter, we will hear of the Dove's Real Beauty programs to counter misplaced judgments about women's appearance and the Dove Self-Esteem program for teens. Neither has any relationship to Dove's business but the effectiveness of the long-term campaign has made it a part of the Dove culture, personality, and image. A fit emerged.

A program can be centered around fundraising. The Avon Walk for Breast Cancer for over 12 years was the centerpiece signature social program for Avon, a skin care and cosmetics firm. The Walk and all that surrounded it—the scheduling, the training, the fund raising (nearly two-thirds of a billion dollars was raised), and the educational impact to well over 100 million women, made it all feel authentic and natural.

There is a choice between an internal, owned program and adopting a nonprofit firm as a signature social program. An internal program can be owned, managed, and resourced by the business. Its fortune is in its hands. But it can be hard to find an internal program opportunity that is "not taken," leverages the firm's assets and resources, is broad enough to be relevant to your business, and is "doable." Even if the program is perfect conceptually, it needs to be implemented right and then staffed, guided, and managed over a long period of time. Not easy.

If the right internal program or programs cannot be found of if they do not exhaust the need for signature programs, an external nonprofit can play a role. It can come with a proven approach, a strong brand, and often can be at scale. The problem is to create a fit and connection that feels right. In Chapter 11, we will see Thrivent, a financial services firm, create a long-term partnership with Habitat for Humanity which involved Thrivent employees and customers in building needed housing around the world. It had nothing to do with the offerings or operations of Thrivent but everything to do with its values, culture, employee experience, and customer connection. The result was a fit with little risk that it would be viewed as only a commercial effort to attract attention and gain respect.

Umbrella brands

In situations where there are multiple signature social programs that combine to represent an entity that has a role in the business strategy, there is a need to create an umbrella brand. That umbrella brand could be the corporate brand itself such as Salesforce (see Chapter 3), a dedicated organizational umbrella brand (see NBA Cares in Chapter 6), a foundation (e.g., the Virgin foundation from Chapter 5), or the grouping of programs (See Chapter 8 where Barclays grouped four programs under the Digital Eagles brand). It is not the case that signature social program has to carry the flag by itself.

An umbrella brand could also be a signature brand in that it is representing another brand in an important way. As a signature brand it may epitomize a dimension of another brand. NBA Cares, for example, represents the societal dimensions of the NBA itself. If there is a question as to the seriousness of the social impact effort of the NBA, NBA Cares is the answer.

More is found in Chapter 6 where the concept of signature social programs is elaborated, internal and external nonprofits are compared, and umbrella branding is discussed. Chapter 7 which has an extended discussion on how to find or create one or more signature programs for your business.

The Future—Integrate Signature Social Programs into a Business

The future needs to do more than establish a signature social program that is on an island required to be self-sufficient. Such an isolated program will not only lack adequate resources, but will be regarded by a sponsoring business as an add-on appendage. As such, it will be a dead weight on the organization taking resources away from needed strategy and tactical investments and thus vulnerable to downturns or new firm leadership.

Instead, the signature social program should be integrated into the business strategy. It should be known and valued within the business and have a blended purpose (or mission), vision, and culture. The signature program strategy should link to the business perceptually, draw on the staff and resources of the business, and integrate its communication message with the communication effort of the business. The two should be part of the same team.

The glue of the integration process is the symbiotic relationship between a business and its adopted partner, a signature social program. Each will materially help the other.

- **A signature program enhances the business.**
- **A business supports a signature program.**

It is a win-win. Further, there is the "flywheel" momentum generated when the business enhancement creates more support for the signature program which then creates more business enhancement and the process repeats. An evaluation of the signature social program that fails to consider all the ways that it creates value may make the strategic mistake of undervaluing a program or exaggerating its weakness.

How to get there? To integrate two forces that are usually separate and independent and sometimes with inconsistent or even competitive goals is not easy. It requires resources, innovative strategies, cross-silo teamwork, shared resources, operational talent, and a hybrid culture. None of these are easy or natural but there is a huge upside to getting it right.

The book will showcase several firms that have achieved a high level of business/social integration starting with Unilever and Salesforce in the following two chapters.

A Signature Program Adds Value to a Business

To be clear, Job 1 of the signature social program and its associated signature brand is to address a societal challenge and create a "make a difference" impact. The "second" or Job 2 for the signature social program, often hidden, is to add economic value primarily by enhancing the brand of a sponsoring firm or business by boosting its visibility, image, connection to employees and customers, and ability to counter "bad" publicity. In part, this is accomplished by infusing the firm or business brand with the inspiration and values that come with the signature brand and the energy and visibility that it precipitates. This role works for an external nonprofit that has been adopted by a business as well as an internal program.

Gaining energy, visibility, and an image lift is particularly useful for a brand with offerings that are taken for granted—think milk, a bank, or a detergent.

Such a brand struggles to get noticed and a signature social program can change that. And if the offering is one that has annoyed, such as insurance or a supermarket that has decided to stop selling your favorite item, a signature program can provide an alternative conversation.

The book provides vivid examples as to how a signature social program can give a business an energy and image lift. Lifebuoy, described in the next chapter, was introduced in 1894 as a hygiene hand soap to fight cholera. Drawing on this legacy purpose, Lifebuoy developed the "Help a Child Reach 5" program of improved handwashing in areas without clean water. Three videos describing mothers in three villages that had experienced the program got 44 million views. Barclays, from Chapter 8, regained lost trust when they created and communicated a signature social program, the Digital Eagles, that helped people adjust and thrive in the digital world. Prior conventional ads did nothing to change the trust ditch they had created.

This Job 2 is a particularly important part of the integration of a signature social program into a business. It is, in fact, half of the integration glue. Without this glue, the signature social programs and the entire social effort that they represent would be regarded as resource drains that are annoying and expendable instead of being a helpful partner.

There is a fine line to be walked because getting the signature social program to help a business brand can engender a perception that the effort is cynical and self-serving with the dominant motivation to enhance its image and gain sales. To reduce this risk, the firm or business needs to demonstrate authentic empathy and commitment to the societal problem or issue. It could, for example, support thought leadership or make clear a long-term commitment, one that spans decades and not months.

Chapter 8 elaborates.

A Business Supports a Signature Social Program

A business that enjoys the Job 2 energy and image lift will be motivated to support the signature social program. Such support can be a game-changer. A business that is a committed active signature programs partner can provide an endorsement that generates invaluable credibility for the signature program that is very difficult to achieve by other means. Further, a signature program integrated into a business will be in a position to access its knowledge, budgets, volunteers, offerings, customer base, market knowledge, and media power. Not only will there be permission but the signature program staff will know what is there that would help and who to work with. The right set of business partners can change a bare-bones, have-baked brand-building effort to a professional, well-funded program.

The integration of the signature social program into the business means that the program is no longer an anchor that sucks resources out of a firm's "productive" investments. The signature program by adding economic value, becomes part of the team instead of a burden

This integrated partnership is important for both internal and external signature social brands. Internal brand teams need to create working relationships and channels of communication with the sponsoring business brands, especially their marketing teams, and attempt to integrate the signature program into the business strategy. External nonprofits have the same challenge but they, in addition, first need to recruit and nurture sponsoring business partners, a process that requires effort and patience.

Gaining and actively managing business partners is not easy but the payoff is high. Habitat for Humanity, for example, from chapter 9 convinced Thrivent and 19 other firms to become "legacy sponsors" to partner with Habitat's to provide housing to those around the world that are in need. These firms provided a financial commitment, volunteers, and material that have allowed Habitat and its global mission to experience spectacular growth.

More in Chapter 9.

Blending the Teams Increases the Payoff

The big payoff comes when the signature program team and the business team are blended. There is cross-organization channels of communication, relationships, projects, task forces, common goals, and shared interests.

Employees of the business will feel more pride and more professional meaning in there work when they are fully informed and even more when they are engaged as part of the effort. And signature program team will feel more confidence, experience more learning, and perform at a higher level when they are part of a combined team that includes needed skills and assets.

The Future—Build Inspiring, Credible Signature Social Brands

For all this to work, for the signature social program to do its jobs of creating impact and enhancing a business brand, it needs to build a strong signature social brand that will provide guidance, clarity, credibility, visibility, and inspiration. All are needed. In addition, Jobs 1 and 2 require communication based on a strong brand.

Note that an umbrella brand can play a signature role at least for some audiences. When that is the case, it will have the same communication tasks as that of a signature social brand and the same need for active brand building. That means that it requires an organizational brand-building home and budget which may not be currently adequate.

How do you go about this brand-building task besides enlisting the support of a business partner? There are roadblocks.

One problem is that social programs, whether internal or external, are often not staffed with people who have a branding background or even have access to those that do. Further, the staff usually have a lot on their plates and little resource slack, so branding does not get the priority it should. The value of the integration with the firm or business is thus even more visible because integration enables the signature program to access the needed talent, budgets, and communication assets.

Another related problem is that signature program staff will believe that the most efficient and effective communication is to use facts and descriptions of program elements and goals. That is usually erroneous and leads to wasteful efforts. What may be needed is a willingness and ability to think out of the box, perhaps creating in-depth stories or even flamboyant stunts to breakthrough, approaches that require getting out of a comfort zone that is not easy.

Brand building has a host of tools, concepts, and vehicles. There are segmentation strategies, positioning strategies, value propositions, points of differentiation, a brand vision, brand personalities, brand communities, and much more. Vehicles can include websites, social media, publicity stunts, blogs, podcasts, newsletters taglines, posters, and advertising. Knowing of these concepts and vehicles is not enough. Each is powerful but only if implemented with professional skill and breakthrough creativity. It is not just about spending money.

In Chapter 10, some fundamentals of brand building are reviewed including some of these concepts and vehicles. In addition, the book introduces in Chapters 11 to 15. five branding "must dos" which are often underused and sometimes unknown or ignored.

Five Branding "Must Dos"

Create a brand North Star to guide and inspire. It should include a brand purpose/mission, vision, position, and tagline. The purpose or mission provides a compact portrayal of the essence of the signature social program. The vision provides the small set of brand pillars representing what the brand stands for. The position guides the communication priorities. The tagline provides a punchy reminder of the brands essence for an external audience. Together they provide a "North Star" for the signature social program, a feeling for what is on and off brand, a direction for enhancing or augmenting the program, and guidance on priorities for operations, budgets and especially communication efforts. When on target, they will resonate and even inspire, differentiate, energize, neutralize competitor advantages, and provide credibility. Chapter 11 elaborates.

Create brand communities A powerful way to connect is to foster brand communities. These are groups of people that share interests, activities, problems, or opinions, with the brand being an active member of the group. This community provides functional information and social benefits. It is a place where experiences, stories and ideas can be shared with others. The brand website becomes the central organizing node and information source. Salesforce, for example, from Chapter 3, has more than 40 nonprofit and higher-education focused user communities around the world that are supported, financed, and managed by Salesforce. These Salesforce "success" communities provide a trusted environment for customers, partners, and prospects to get answers, share ideas, collaborate, and learn best practices. The social and functional experience can bind people to a brand more than any communication program. More on brand communities in Chapter 12.

Use stories. Beware of disinterest and counterarguing undercutting your communication efforts. The painful truth is that people, in a time in which media clutter and information overload is overwhelming, are not interested in your facts or program descriptions. They have other ways to spend their time. If they do process your facts or descriptions, they will be skeptical. Into that that environment, come stories that research shows have the ability to attract attention, gain involvement, create emotional connections, engender positive feelings, resist counter-arguing, and be remembered. The goal should be to find "signature" stories that have a WOW factor with an exceptional ability to entertain, inform, intrigue, or involve. Chapter 13 explains the why and how of stories.

Develop and use silver bullet brands. A silver bullet brand is a brand that helps another brand by providing energy, differentiation, or credibility. It can be a feature, service, founder, story, or endorser that provides an answer to the question—"why this program?" If you ask why people are drawn to your brand, and the answer is not branded, you may have missed an opportunity. If your "secret sauce" were branded, it would have the status of being "worth branding," be easier to communicate, and most importantly, would be ownable. Chapter 14 provides case studies of silver bullets in action.

Scale the program. If the program is successful at achieving real impact, consideration should be given to scaling it, so it can be replicated it to other geographies or target audiences. It may be possible to make the core idea ten times, a hundred times, or a thousand times more impactful. One way to scale is to become a partner, consultant, or the provider of support for others who want to address the same social need and could benefit from knowing how it is done. Scaling, turning local success in much more, can be difficult to staff and resource given the day-to-day needs of a program, but it is a route to a home-run impact. Chapter 15 has more.

Each of these can change the fortunes of a signature social program by supporting its brand strategy and brand activation.

The Role of Branding

Branding, its concepts and tools, play a central role in creating social program leadership and an effective "business/social" strategy. It is brands that make the firm's societal effort create synergies and clarity instead of being ad hoc and confusing. Branding is too often underappreciated, under resourced, and/ or inadequately implemented in the social program world. To see the role of branding up close, we reprise the strategic thrusts through a branding lens.

Attack society challenges with signature social programs. Just the idea that a signature social program is needed to communicate the commitment of a firm or business to societal challenges to employees and other stakeholders is a significant branding decision. The selection of the societal need and responsive program requires a feel for what will resonate and what will fit the firm or business, both require a branding perspective. A purpose or mission of a firm or business is a cornerstone of its brand and adapting or augmenting it to make societal challenges thus affects the brand. Further, organizational culture is driven in large part by the organizational brand, its implementation, and communication.

Integrating signature social programs into a business. Others have suggested that a social effort will help a business but have not explicitly observed that a primary route is by elevating and strengthening the business brand. That route requires an understanding of what the brand equity of a firm or business brand consists of—namely visibility, image, and stakeholder loyalty—and how the inspiration and credibility of a signature social program might affect it.

Building inspiring, credible signature social brands. The signature social brand is the driver of the program's social impact and its ability to enhance a business and therefore needs to be strong. That means branding concepts and tools such as positioning, a brand vision, brand communities, signature stories, websites, social media, podcasts, being endorsed by a firm or business and more need to be accessed at a high level.

Brand Portfolio Synergy

The signature social brand is part of a brand portfolio or brand family. There are four sets of brand relationship that need to be managed to ensure that they create synergy and not confusion and inefficiencies.

The business partner. The signature social brand has a relationship with the sponsoring business each influencing and benefiting the other that needs to be actively managed. In addition the link between the two needs to be established. In particular, the business brand should cue the signature brand.

Other signature programs. There are almost always other, sometimes many, such signature social programs. The challenge is to manage this team to make sure that there are clarity of roles, potential brand-building synergies are achieved, opportunities to expand impact are pursued, and resources allocation among the programs is strategic. Umbrella brands have a strategic role to play and should be understood.

The signature programs silver bullet brands or "secret sauce." These are branded features, services, stories, founders, or endorsers that need to be managed, resourced, and linked to the signature brand. More in Chapter 14.

Outside partner brands. Outside organizations such as the Girl Scouts can support or leverage a signature brand with a relevant mission. As we shall see in Chapter 12, Patagonia's social effort involves several industry organizations with similar goals.

The Book Plan

The book will discuss why each of these strategic thrusts need to be understood and also how to be successfully implemented. The book has four parts.

Part I The Context

The three chapters of Part I (chapters 2, 3, and 4) will provide a context to better understand the role of social programs. The first two of these chapters present case studies of two role model firms. The first, Unilever, is a diversified BtoC (business to consumer) firm, over a century old, with over a hundred strong brands marketed around the world. The second, Salesforce, is a BtoB (business to business) company that's just over two decades old with offerings under a single brand. These two illustrate the power of social programs; the complexity created by multiple and varied programs, societal needs, and stakeholders; and the power of integrating the social effort into the business.

The third chapter of Part I (chapter 4), will show that firm's social efforts have moved from "nice to have" to being a "must have" by analyzing five forces—the emergence of the stakeholder business paradigm; the visibility of society's problems and issues; the unique ability of firms to make meaningful impact on these problems and issues, pressure from employees, customers, and investors; and the needs of business brands that for an energy and image lift. The battle is not over and there is enormous upside still on the table, but the momentum is surging.

Part II Signature Social Programs

Part II, presents the rationale for the first strategic thrust, the signature social program and the challenges it represents.

- Chapter 5 explains how a purpose/mission and culture can enable signature social programs to be developed and thrive.
- Chapter 6 defines signature social programs and presents the internal vs external options.
- Chapter 7 discusses how to find or create signature social programs and suggests choice criteria.

Part III—Integrating the Signature Social Program into a Business.

Part III discusses the second strategic thrust, the integration of the signature program into a business strategy and the how the program enhances and received support from a business.

- Chapter 8 details how a signature social program can give a business brand a lift and why that should and can be done.
- Chapter 9 shows how a business can help a brand plus how to blend two organizations together.

Part IV—Putting Signature Social Brand on Steroids—5 Branding "Must Dos"

The remaining imperative, the subject of Part IV, puts us in the shoes of the signature social program leadership. How can they, with the help of a business partner, build a vigorous, strong brand, a brand which can help in impacting a societal need, representing a firm's social efforts, and enhancing a business brand?

Chapter 10 reviews some proven brand-building concepts and tools.

In chapters 11 to 16, five branding "must dos" are presented—creating a North Star direction, brand communities, signature stories, silver bullet brands, and ways to scale an effective program.

The book has been written for firms that are committed to a meaningful societal effort and to nonprofits that would like to be the signature social program for nonprofits organizations looking for program partners. The goal is to reach and help both by providing insights into how branding concepts and tools can help them create and manage programs that address societal needs that are both real and feel real, while also helping build the brand of a partnering business.

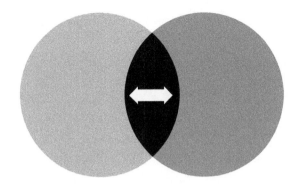

Part I
Purpose-Driven Branding—
The Context

In Part I, a context will be presented that will help motivate and illustrate the material in Part II, III, and IV where the essence of the "future of purpose-driven branding" will be set forth. Two case studies, that of Unilever and Salesforce presented in Chapters 2 and 3, will show the complexity of purpose-driven branding and the potential payoff of getting it right. In chapter 4, the five forces driving the momentum toward elevating social efforts in business strategy and priorities which is making such efforts "must haves" rather than "nice to have" will be presented. Understanding these forces is necessary if organizational support for social programs is to flourish.

Chapter 2

UNILEVER—A HERITAGE OF ADDRESSING SOCIETY NEEDS

How selfish soever man may be supposed, there are evidently some principles in his nature which interest him in the fortune of others, and render their happiness necessary to him, though he derives nothing from it except the pleasure of seeing it.

Adam Smith in "Theory of Moral Sentiment"
written before "The Wealth of Nations"

The Unilever Story

In 1894, soap maker William Hesketh Lever, introduced Lifebuoy Soap. Its mission was to combat cholera in Victorian England and make health and hygiene accessible to everyone—its tag was "For preservation of health." It was the start of the Lever Brothers.

Lever was way ahead of his time with respect to having a social mission.[1] He advocated profit sharing which he labeled as "prosperity sharing," built a model city for employees named Port Sunlight (whose homes are still sought after today), campaigned for benefits to the elderly, provided schooling and healthcare for palm oil plantations in the Congo, and promoted the health benefits of handwashing to all. It was not all about profits for Lever in the era of Carnegie, Vanderbilt, Rockefeller, and others who did not share his values.

In 1930 Lever Brothers, a UK firm, merged with a Dutch company, Margarine Unie. The combined company became Unilever and embarked on an ambitious program of acquiring businesses and brands including early investments in frozen food, and shampoo. In 2021, it was a 60-billion-dollar company operating in 190 countries with over 400 brands under the "Purpose Led, Future Fit" business model with a strategy that in part involved "win with our brands as a force for good powered by purpose and innovation."[2]

In the 1990s and early 2000s, Unilever was making sharp improvements in delivering products that promote health and wellbeing and in the forefront of environmental efforts. From 1995 to 2010, the firm had reduced the CO2 emissions (per unit of production) by 44%, its water usage by 66% and the total waste by 73%. It was recognized globally for its efforts. For example, it was the top firm by a healthy margin in the 2010 Dow Jones Sustainability Index for the drink and food super-sector in the annual Globescan study in which 700 experts across the globe were asked name the firms that were sustainability leaders.[3]

Unilever in 2010 with considerable momentum already in place put its social effort on steroids and gave it a brand name, **Unilever Sustainable Living Program (USLP)**. The firm's and the USLP purpose became "to make sustainable living commonplace" believing that this is the best long-term way for the business to grow. The umbrella brand USLP helped communicate internally and externally the priority and substance behind its purpose. It because a signature brand for Unilever because it was an important proof point for its effort to address the challenges facing society.

The architect and energy behind this effort was a new 52-year-old CEO that joined the firm in 2009. Paul Polman, who was to become the most visible corporate spokesperson for the concept that shareholders should not be the only stakeholder of importance and maximizing profits should not be the only objective in a world that needs business to become an active partner in addressing environmental and social challenges.

Growing up on England with five siblings, Polman came to the US in 1979 and got his MBA at the University of Cincinnati while beginning his 27-year stint at P&G working in maintenance to finance his schooling. During his P&G career, he experienced the economic value of social initiatives like taking waste out of a Belgium detergent factory. He also saw their ability to foster growth. As president of global fabrics at P&G in the early 2000s he talked about the business opportunities created by programs to address poverty, disease, nutrition, and the quality of women's lives. After a varied and successful P&G career, he moved to Nestle for four years where, after being passed over for its CEO job, he became available for Unilever.

Signaling his priorities at Unilever, one of Polman's first decisions was to stop earnings guidance before quarterly profit reports reflecting his interest in moving attention away from short-term financials and toward a long-term value model of business which, in his words, "is equitable, is shared, and is sustainable."[4] He noted that "our purpose is to have a sustainable business model that is put in the service of the greater good."[5] He invited investors that do not buy into this business model to put their money in other firms.

The rationale as explained by Polman is fascinating. He noted that because of the limits of capitalism we have created an unsustainable set of problems which include global warming, resource depletion, and an increasing gap between the rich and poor. He then said that "business has to decide what role it wants to play. Does it sit on the sidelines waiting for governments to take action or does it get on the pitch (the center of a cricket playing field) and start addressing these issues? In Unilever we believe that business must be part of the solution. But to be so, business will have to change. It will have to get off the treadmill of quarterly reporting and operate for the long term. It will have to see itself as part of society, not separate from it. And it will have to recognize that the needs of citizens and communities carry the same weight as the demands of shareholders."[6]

Unilever Sustainable Living Plan—USLP Followed by Unilever Compass

The Unilever Sustainable Living Plan (USLP) involved a ten-year journey towards sustainable growth and was followed by a second ten-year commitment,

Unilever Compass. USLP evolved over the years but is organized into three thrusts that focused on:

- **Improving the health of the planet.** Generate products and programs that reduce greenhouse gases, conserve water, reduce waste in general (especially plastic waste), and promote sustainable sourcing. Advocate for public policy positions that will conserve resources and protect the planet.
- **Improving health, confidence, and wellbeing.** Make foods that are healthier. Create programs that reduce hunger, provide safer water, reduce disease, instill confidence, and improve the sense of wellbeing. Take stands for social policies that will enhance lives.
- **Contributing to a fairer and more inclusive world.** Stand up for human rights, fair treatment of employees, meaningful work, equality and diversity in the workplace, and practice ethical behavior.

Several observations. First, the word "sustainable" in USLP, and in many if not most contexts, goes beyond an environmental focus to include programs to improve health, confidence, and wellbeing plus policies that promote inclusion and fairness in society. A sustainable strategy will involve all social programs. It implies a long-term focus looking to serve future generations, it is not about monthly financials.

Second, all the three areas are very broad in scope and mission. Improving health, confidence and wellbeing, for example, has four categories of programs with labels: Equality and Inclusion, Raising Living Standards, Positive Nutrition, and Health & Well-Being. And each of these has subcategories. The Health & Well-Being category, for example, incudes Sanitary & Hygiene, Oral Hygiene, Self Esteem, and Brand Driven Inclusion. These subcategories, such as Health & Well-Being, could be considered a signature subbrand under the USLP umbrella brand depending on who the audience is.

Because the USLP mission represents a broad umbrella, each of the 400 brands in each of the 190 countries can create products and social programs that fit their context. Those that are effective, and especially those that directly and indirectly promote an Unilever business, can be scaled to other countries and sometimes other products.

Third, measurable goals provide momentum and urgency to these three broad areas. Unilever put into place more than 50 time-bound measures to guide programs from the sourcing of raw materials all the way through to the use of products in the home. The emphasis on measurement is based upon a recognition that firms and people respond to what is measured. Quantifying progress leads to the evaluation and improvement of initiatives and programs. Even if the measures are imperfect, they still provide an useful perspective.

Sustainable Living Brands. In 2010, it was recognized that of their 400 brands some brands already performed well with respect to USLP. These brands were awarded the label of a Sustainable Living Brand, defined as a brand that "communicate a strong environmental or social purpose, with products that contribute to achieving the company's ambition of halving its environmental footprint and increasing its positive social impact."[7] Each year more were added as they qualified.

By 2020 there were 28 Sustainable Living Brands at Unilever, up from 17 only three years before, that included not only Dove, Lifebuoy, Ben & Jerry's which will be described shortly but also:

- OMO, with Outdoor Classroom Day has stimulated outdoor play activities for children under the "dirt is good" tagline.
- Vaseline, which has reached 3 million people living on the frontline of poverty and disaster with skin healing program, Equitable Skincare for All.
- Knorr, who attacked iron-deficiency anemia in Nigeria with its Knorr Force For Good Program with a fortified bouillon cube and a campaign to put green in recipes.
- Lipton Tea, with a purpose that includes: "nature has been our tea factory. Every cup of Lipton tea is grown using natural rain, wind, and sunshine to give you our signature rich taste and aroma" has made significant efforts to protect the rain forest initiatives.
- Seventh Generation, with its plant-based cleaning products that aims to "inspire a consumer revolution that nurtures the health of the next seven generations."

The USLP performance between 2010 and 2021 is very impressive and widely recognized. During that decade, Unilever dominated the top spot in the Globescan study. Its stock went from 20 to 60 and the Sustainable Living Brands saw substantially more growth than the other Unilever brands.[8]

A few random snapshots of the societal impact of the USLP effort.[9]

Environmental action. The CO_2 emissions were reduced by 65% from 2008 to 2019. By 2019 24 plants were carbon neutral, products were redesigned to conserve energy (some products were made more concentrated for example) and 100% of the grid electricity use came from renewables. The plastic waste problem was attacked with recycling infrastructure investments, product redesign and an ambitious goal to reduce the use of plastic and increase further recycling by 2025. The total waste footprint was reduced 32% from 2010 to 2019. In addition, the percent of agricultural sources that were sustainable went from 14% in 2010 to 62% in 2019.

Improving health. Across the company, there were initiatives to provide plant-based products, which are an important component of creating a sustainable food system and reducing global warming--from Hellman's vegan mayonnaise to Ben and Jerry's dairy-free ice cream. Initiatives to reduce the sugar and salt content and fortify food products are ongoing. From 2010 to 2019, Unilever helped 1.3 billion people improve their health and hygiene through better handwashing, toilet innovations, and safer water.

People's self-confidence. Employees were encouraged to participate in the "People with Purpose" campaign in which they addressed some probing questions leading to the articulation of a persona by participants. Labels such as "Human Spark Ignitor," "Disruptive Digital Leader," or "Green Planet Savior" emerged—Nearly 50,000 discovered their purpose in the half decade after the program started in 2014.

Toward a fairer world. Under the Framework for Fair Compensation Initiative, progress was made to make sure there is gender equality and a livable wage throughout the firms operations. The Responsible Source Policy sets standards on human and labor rights for suppliers. In 2019, 70% met those requirements. Throughout the world efforts were made to encourage women entrepreneurs.

USLP had a ten-year planning horizon. In 2019, Polman was followed in a CEO role by Alan Jope, a 35-year Unilever employee who had held several key Unilever executive roles around the world. Jope doubled down on USLP with the Unilever Compass, which used the same three thrusts of USLP with extended programs, ambitious new goals, and renewed energy. It represented an enhanced commitment to the societal challenges facing the firm and the world. In his words, "At the heart of the Unilever Compass is a belief that sustainable and purposeful business drives superior long-term performance by connecting with the billions of people around the world we serve who want to see companies and brands step-up and actively engage in addressing today's most urgent and deep-seated societal challenges, not just pay them lip service."[10]

Jope went on--"The power and relevance of the Unilever Compass was captured vividly in 2020 in the launch of some major initiatives. Clean Future, for example, commits us to replace all of the fossil fuel-derived carbon in our cleaning and laundry products with renewable or recycled carbon by 2030. And with Future Foods, we have set an ambition to transform the global food system, reduce food waste and accelerate the move to plant-based meat and dairy alternatives."[11] Both could be signature programs. These and an extensive set of others, all are under the expanded mission—"We aim to make sustainable living commonplace with high-performing brands that are a force for good, taking action for a more sustainable and equitable world."[12]

Let's take a closer look at three of these Sustainable Living brands Dove, Lifebuoy, and Ben & Jerry's to see how the Unilever Compass (USLP) works at the brand level.

Dove—Elevating Women's Confidence and Self-Esteem

In 1955, Unilever introduced the Dove "beauty bar" (not a soap) containing a patented, mild, moisturization ingredient that generated a noticeably different "feel" to the skin based on research during World War II on non-irritant wound cleaners. It was positioned as having one-fourth cleansing cream that "creams" skin while washing (as opposed to a soap that would dry your skin while removing dirt and grease). The cleansing cream became a "moisturizer cream" and was shown being poured into the beauty bar.

By 2004, Dove had expanded to 80 countries and was having a harder time differentiating its brand and growing the business in part because it had expanded to new product areas such as body wash, shampoo, deodorants, and other offerings where moisturizing was less relevant and in part because of competition. They needed a new positioning strategy and began basic research on perceived beauty.

Dove's research suggested that women had a distorted view of their appearance because of a mythical "ideal" that led to a "real beauty" study of 3,200 women. It revealed the extent of the problem--only 12% believed they were above average and just 2% believed they were beautiful. Even children were affected by a poor appearance self-image which led to emotional and behavioral problems.

As a result, in 2004, Dove introduced a new social mission, to redefine "Real Beauty" to help women view their body image positively. The Campaign for Real Beauty started with advertisements showing real women who may have been older or heavier than the "ideal," but exhibited beauty. Billboard ads invited passers-by to vote on whether a particular model was, for example, "Fat or Fab" or "Wrinkled or Wonderful," with the results of the votes dynamically updated. It hit a nerve. Over one million voted on the Dove website and sales of Dove products were 6% over the prior year.

One of its early ads, Evolution, showed how much make-up effort and digital alteration goes behind creating what is an "artificial model look." The ad garnered 170 million views on YouTube in a month and created unpaid exposure, estimated to be worth more than $150 million.[13]

A series of campaigns kept making the same point, each woman is more beautiful than her self-image and should believe in herself. In one 2013 campaign, a forensic sketch artist drew several women, first based only on their descriptions of themselves (he does not actually see them) and then based on the descriptions of a stranger who had observed the women. In the ad, the subject realizes that the sketches inspired by strangers are much more flattering than those based on their own self-descriptions. The tagline? "You are more beautiful than you think." In another campaign, women who wore a "confidence" patch felt and acted more confident and then were stunned to learn the patch contained nothing. In still another, in five major global cities women had two doors to select when entering a store, one marked beautiful and the other average. A discussion ensued—Why did so many not chose the beautiful door? These three efforts earned 14 billion global impressions and had an estimated ROI of $4.42 for every dollar spent.

The early success of "Real Beauty" encouraged Dove executives to go beyond advertising that called attention to the problem and into creating meaningful programs that more proactively did something about it. The result was the **Dove Self Esteem** program with a focus on 11-14 -old girls. It was based in part on research that found, for example, that 8 out of 10 girls are so concerned with the way they look that they opt out of important activities. Its mission became helping "the next generation grow up enjoying a positive relationship with the way they look, to help them raise their self-esteem and realize their full potential."[14]

The Self-Esteem program has many branded supporting programs, all influenced by experts in addressing the self-judgmental issues of teen and preteen girls. It provides guides to teachers (**Confident Me**), parents (**Uniquely Me**) and to youth leaders (**True to Me**). There is a "girls room" five episode series where a girl's bathroom mirror experience is linked to barriers to self-esteem. An annual **Dove Self-Esteem Weekend**. supported by discussion aids, aims to inspire moms and mentors to talk to the girls in their lives about beauty, confidence, and self-esteem. And a series of six one-minute animations on body image supplemented by downloadable comic books and workshops for 7 to 10 year old's reached over 20 million kids in two years. These are candidates to be signature subbrands under the Dove Self-Esteem program.

Dove recognized the need to partner with organizations that understand girl issues to scale ideas and programs. It has long collaborated with World Association of Girl Guides and Girl Scouts which represent 10 million girls. One result was the "Free Being Me" self-confidence program that reached 4.6 million girls in the first five years. The program and others were inspired by primary research on young women and the issues they face. "Free Being Me" uses fun, interactive activities to teach young people that body confidence and self-esteem come from valuing their bodies, standing up to social pressures, and supporting others to be more body confident. The presence in some 150 countries allowed for innovation and experimentation to flourish. When something worked in one country it adapted for other countries.

Dove employees and partners became involved starting in 2008. Eight years later over 3,000 employees and partners had conducted body confidence activities reaching over 30,000 young people. This involvement reflected the impact that the program had internally on the culture and strategy of the brand. And some gave talks. The Global Director of Dove Self-Esteem Program, Meaghan Ramsey gave a TED talk on "Why Thinking Your're Ugly Is Bad for You" that received over 4 million views, a major brand-builder for Dove and for the Dove Self-Esteem Program.

These social programs worked. In addition to gaining visibility for the problem, it changed perceptions and attitudes. Some careful experiments on the target audience revealed that self-images and concerns about appearance were affected not only right after being exposed to one of the campaigns but also months later.[15] In 2021, Dove reported that The Dove Self-Esteem Project reached over 60 million young people with self-esteem education, and by 2030, the aim is to have helped 250 million build their positive body image.

The new social mission elevated the brand and the business. An intent-to-purchase rose by between 10 and 25 percentage points when people were aware of the self-esteem activities. Dove sales went from $2,5 billion in 2004 to $6 billion in 2018.[16] An internal Dove study found that those countries that spent aggressively on these social programs had double the growth compared to those that spent little or nothing on them. Dove thrived and its social programs were largely responsible.

The AXE problem. AXE is a brand of male grooming products that was launched in France in 1983 by Unilever and is marketed in over 90 countries, some under the brand Lynx. From the 1990s, AXE was positioned as the brand that would help men, even geeky men, attract women. A scent from AXE would make gorgeous women swoon over the man smart enough to wear it. The commercials were over-the-top outrageous and humorous but the message was clear, the AXE scent was a powerful attraction to desirable women. AXE was a huge commercial success. The target market watched the humorous ads and resonated, perhaps unconsciously (as opposed to rationally) to the message.

AXE led to the accusation that Unilever was being hypocritical. How could the firm allow AXE to run communications so degrading to women while Dove was preaching about "real beauty" and self-esteem. How can any organization stand behind both routes to a customer relationship? It was a tough question that was to follow Unilever for many years and since AXE was an autonomous brand, albeit not a Sustainable Living brand, the solution was illusive.

AXE in 2016 realized that in addition to the internal pressure to stop contributing "social harm," their market had changed and the traditional AXE appeal started to be an anachronism acting as an anchor rather than being a growth driver.

Two studies and a film were influential.[17] The first study, in 2014, involved over 3,000 men in 10 countries and showed that men feel overwhelming pressure to conform to outdated notions of masculinity. Another study in 2015, found that 9 out of 10 women prefer men that are comfortable being themselves. The 90-minute film "The Mask You Live In" followed boys and young men who were pressured by the media, their peers, and even adults to conform to long-established masculine stereotypes. They faced pressures to disconnect from their emotions, devalue true friendships, objectify women and use violence. The movie added expert commentary from psychologists and others, plus empirical evidence, to support tactics to combat it. AXE later became a partner and sponsor of this powerful film.

The result was a new Axe effect—to empower men to express their individuality, becoming their most attractive selves. And to break down the masculinity labels and assumptions that have been created over decades of stereotyping. It was supported by a broader range of male grooming products and advertising that in a series of stories told how men could be as attractive as they could be—themselves. Under the theme "Find your magic," it showed the power of individualism, being yourselves and not confirming to expectations of being "masculine."

Among the AXE initiatives was a partnership with the **Ditch the Label** organization to help men fight the incidence of being pigeonholed or bullied by the use of labels. Labels can influence how a boy or man perceives himself and how he treats others. One study showed that 3 in 4 guys had been called names for the way they look, whether that's in the workplace or in schools. Very provocative and disturbing.

The new AXE became a Sustainable Living Brand at Unilever in 2017 and the embarrassing inconsistency was no longer on the table. The brand developed a mission that included a social dimension, to build the self-confidence of men and boys.

Lifebuoy: A Life Saving Social Program

Since its launch in 1894 as the "Royal Anti-Germ" soap with a mission to combat cholera, Lifebuoy has focused on encouraging people to wash their hands properly to maintain good health, and hygiene. During World War I, the firm encouraged non-combatants to send Lifebuoy soap to soldiers to help protect them from disease. Over a century later, its aim is still to save lives through handwashing with soap. The Lifebuoy mission in 2021 is to "make a difference by creating quality, affordable products and promoting healthy hygiene habits."

During the early 2000s, there was an active Lifebuoy campaign in India to encourage handwashing the hygienic way in part to reduce the number of kids that failed to reach their fifth birthday, some 2 million globally. Prior research showed that effective handwashing with soap at key occasions during the day can reduce deadly diseases like diarrhea by 45% and pneumonia by 23% worldwide, the primary causes of children's deaths. A study of the Lifebuoy program in Thesgora, a 1,500-home diarrhea-prone Indian village showed even better results with a reduction in diarrhea from 36% to 6%, which helped Unilever decide to accelerate program expansion.

The Lifebuoy team was finding it hard to get traction for the program even with aggressive efforts in communicating what the program was and its amazing results. Frustrated by the difficulty of breaking through, Samir Singh, then the head of Lifebuoy worldwide, held a brainstorming session with the brand team from Lifebuoy and their ad agency. The brief that emerged was extreme--to dramatize the death of one child as opposed to communicating the program. The result was the idea to tell the story of a parent who lost a child or was one of the lucky ones. It was clear they had a winning idea and test results showed it.

There were several notable outcomes. One was a brand name, "Help a Child Reach 5" that vividly told about the tragic reality regarding the death of young children and how that could be avoided.[18] The name said it all, but some background data and program information made it even more impactful. Second, the handwashing program was refined with added features. Third, a series of powerful impactful stories that broke through the clutter and provided enormous energy. Finally, support was received for the decision to scale the programs throughout India and in 24 other countries.

In 2013, the "Help a Child Reach 5" campaign was launched with a mission to save lives by spreading the importance of good handwashing habits around the world. It became an impressive program by its scope in terms of the countries it reached, its long-term perspective, its well- conceived components, and its measurable impact. Not incidentally, the program was also effective at increasing the visibility, respect and sales of the Lifebuoy brand. A snapshot of the efforts:

- To reach school children, five superheroes **(the School of Five)** Biff, Pow, Barn, Hairyback, and Sparkel come to life to tell kids how to handwash, why it is critical to do so, and to highlight the five occasions during the day that handwashing is the most important (a device that illuminates germs after a hand wash illustrates). The content comes to life in animations, radio shows, music, games, and school visits.
- Young people are enlisted. The **Lifebuoy Lifesaver Volunteer Program** harnesses the energy and enthusiasm of teenagers and college students to run Lifebuoy's School of Five programing in schools. By 2019, more than 150,000 were mobilized. Over 140,000 girl scouts in India became handwashing heroes by promoting this lifesaving habit within their local communities. In Kenya, students volunteer to be **"Heroes for Change."**
- Over 40,000 Lifebuoy employees have volunteered to support the program.
- The phrase "Did you wash your hands with Lifebuoy today?" was put on over 2.5 million pieces of flatbread called "rotis" during a Hindu holiday.
- Measurement--daily dairies provided a key measurement of the impact of the various program touchpoints guiding refinement and reallocation.

Three videos that described emotional stories about the impact of the program on Thesgora and two other Indian villages through the eyes of the parents of an affected child got an astounding 45 million views on YouTube alone. That, for a bar soap!

In a Thesgora video we see a father walking on his hands through fields, puddles, and a stairway to the nearby temple to seek God's blessing because his boy reached five. Real village people follow him, some playing music. We see the boy with love toward his father in his eyes. The father is clearly overcome with delight about this birthday and we learn that the boy is the first child that the boy's grandfather has seen reach five.

In another video, we are introduced to Utari a women obsessed by a tree. She waters it, dances by it, shoos away water buffalo, places a ribbon around it, and stays with it into the night. Her husband advises her to go to bed because tomorrow is a big day, the fifth birthday of their son. We learn at this village a tree is planted when a child is born and that Utari has only a tree left because her child died. The video closes with an explanation why the Lifebuoy hand-washing program works to reduce such deaths.

In the third, Samgrahe a young mother from a village with bad sanitation, is seeing a video made 6 years into the future showing her adorable daughter, Chamki, playing and going to school. She is thanking her mom for creating for her a purple frock, making her laugh, and getting her to wash hands even when others made fun of her because that meant Chamki avoided the sickness that took the life of others in her village.

The "Help a Child Reach 5" program's goal was to reach 1 billion people by 2020 with the message that good handwashing habits are necessary and can prevent many of the deaths of kids under 5 that occur each year. The goal was reached two years early either by on the ground contact or by media messaging.

The effectiveness of the program is impressive. In one study, new mothers who took part in the program were more likely to wash their hands with soap than the control group during three occasions: after changing nappies (26% vs 2%), before breastfeeding (42% vs 3%), and after visiting the toilet (39% vs 10%). In addition, 90% of the new mothers reached talked about the program to their friends, family, and neighbors, highlighting a positive ripple effect.

The "Help a Child Reach 5" program was joined by other programs designed to help advance the handwashing cause with different populations and countries with different methods that did not fit the "Help A Child Reach 5" regimen. Among them were:

- A **"mothers" program**. Mothers are contacted via the ubiquitous mobile phone with advice about their baby's health and information about hand-washing. The effort includes letting moms know if there is an infection active in the area. More than 20 million mothers across Asia and Africa have been reached since 2011 with hygiene education through community visits and neonatal clinics.

- **A H is for Handwashing program** provided a tool to introduce handwashing habit to preschool youngsters who are learning the letters of the alphabet.

- **Access to clean water** is inhibiting the hygiene effort and Lifebuoy is working with partners to improve water access.

- **The Super School of Five program** was launched in 2015 in Kenya in partnership with Sightsavers (better handwashing can reduce the risk of Trachoma which can lead to blindness in the vulnerable under 10 population by 30%). By 2020, it had extended to other countries and was in 300 schools. It is a 21-day program involving a pledge, hand washing stations, activities, games, songs, competitions and a completion certificate.

- **Global Handwashing Day** with Lifebuoy as a founding partner, was established in 2008. Almost 100 influencers, including actors and athletes with a reach of over 3.6 million people around the world, were recruited by Lifebuoy to amplify the handwashing message with soap. The annual event has grown to where in one day in October, over 500 million people in 100 countries joined to celebrate handwashing.[19]

- **Gavi, the Vaccine Alliance**, was used to raise awareness of the power of immunization combined with handwashing with soap to accelerate child survival outcomes.

The last two are external signature programs that work alone side "Help a Child Reach 5" and service to increase its visibility and impact. They are good examples of a win-win partnership and the blend of internal and external programs.

Lifebuoy became one of Unilever's fastest-growing brands with compound annual growth of 9.6% from 2008 to 2018, in large part from its association with the hand washing program.[20] In 2020, Lifebuoy was the world's number one selling germ protection soap. In the Kanter Brand Footprint survey involving over 21,000 FMCG (fast moving consumer goods) brands in 49 countries, Lifebuoy was number five in terms of penetration and usage after Coca-Cola, Colgate, Maggi and Lay's.[21]

Ben & Jerry's

In 1978, childhood friends Jerry Greenfield and Ben Cohen, after completing a correspondence course on ice cream, opened an ice cream parlor in Burlington, Vermont out of a renovated gas station. They offered their own ice cream, specializing in additive chunks to provide texture. Early on, their unique personality with their humor, attitude and social concern was apparent.

One of their values was to have fun. That led to creative flavors, often fan suggested, like Cherry Garcia (Grateful Dead), Karmel Sutra (Imagine whirled peace), Magic Brownie (Jimmy Fallon's snack), Hillary Rocky Roadham Clinton, and Phish Food. And the Vermonster challenge--20 scoops of ice cream, four sliced bananas, two cookies, two brownies, hot caramel, toppings, all finished off with a massive layer of whipped cream, or the "Cowmobile," a modified mobile home used to distribute free scoops of Ben & Jerry's ice cream in a unique, cross-country adventure.

Another value was to give back to society and their community. A Ben & Jerry's foundation funded by a percent of profits steps up financially to address needs of the community and society. And there were plenty of local initiatives such as a Free Cone Day for local charities, But the signature effort was a passion for societal issues that often resulted in very vocal and often outrageous support of a perceived need or issue that arose. Ben & Jerry's is visible with an opinion often within hours of a precipitating event that brought the need or issue to the surface. Never being afraid of controversy but rather embracing it, their judgments were often outrageously pointed and ambitious.

In June of 2020, for example, Ben & Jerry's issued a statement amid the Black Lives Matter protests prompted by the death of George Floyd in Minneapolis. Entitled "Silence is NOT an Option" its statement stood out from expressions of other firms by its emotion, its specificity, its call to action and its direct reminder that all citizens needed to take responsibility for the core problems.[22] The statement directly called out systemic racism, offered specific suggestions for remedies, promoted relevant articles from their website, and, most of all, created a sense of urgency and a shared responsibility for action. It was typical Ben & Jerry's instinct to be forceful and provocative without compromise.

The Ben & Jerry's social commitment drew on their ability to shake up the conversation with unique stunts. On Earth Day in 2005, when a vote in the U.S. Senate proposed the opening of the Arctic National Wildlife Refuge to oil drilling, Ben & Jerry's launched a protest by creating the largest ever Baked Alaska, weighing 900 pounds and placed it in front of the U.S. Capital Building.

Ben & Jerry's social portfolio was broad with a focus on what was right at the moment. Their highlighted areas included building peace, refugees, climate justice, LGBT equality, fairness, racial justice, democracy, money in politics, and in their own operations packaging (an early mover to paperboard packaging), treating suppliers fairly, CMO labeling, the use of hormones to increase milk output in cows, and fair treatment of suppliers.

Most issues were attacked using a band of partners well positioned to impact. For example, the organization, Fairtrade, sets a fair price to workers and farmers in underdeveloped counters. Ben & Jerry's follows their certified price and pays a price premium to fund improvements in the local communities. The climate justice effort supports the youth-led global climate strike hosted by 350. org. Another partner was the Children's Defense Fund in an effort to highlight children's basic needs resulted in over 70,000 postcards sent to Congress.

Ben & Jerry's, instead of a signature program or need, has a signature style with its irreverent and forceful statements about topical social issues and willingness to create outsized activities or events that are eye-catching. The brand is loud, sometimes obnoxious to some, but it represents two guys that built a business with a social conscious and sense of humor. In 2000, Unilever acquired

Ben & Jerry's with the promise to continue its tradition of fighting to address critical economic and social missions with its unique style.

Ben & Jerry's really has two brands with the same name. One is a business brand with ice cream and a colorful personality. The other is a social brand that focuses on society needs and employs the forceful positions and antics of the two founders with a distinct signature style.

Reflections

Unilever's success at addressing society's challenges and supporting the business models have several lessons. One overall observation is how integrated the business strategy and the signature social programs were. In the Lifebuoy and Dove cases the signature programs were the heart of the branding and marketing effort. For Ben & Jerry's the personality of the firm was defined by the two partners and their signature activities and views. And the Unilever brand made the social purpose a fully integrated part of the business. Some other learnings.

Organizational Support is Needed

A social program will be enabled and enhanced when it has the support of a firm such as Unilever. Without its resources and social purpose these major programs would have struggled.

CEO Level Commitment and visibility. The visibility of the CEO and other executives in creating commitment that leads to substance, continuity, and authenticity. This was demonstrated by William Hesketh Lever at the outset, Paul Polman the leader that created USLP and Alan Jope who followed plus those running Unilever's "big brands." This commitment led to a flow of innovative programs that rather than having a short-term promotional goal, were part of a long-term perspective.

Heritage. Have a heritage going back to a founder story 130 or so years ago that serves to provide credibility for programs related to health and to represent the commitment and values of the Unilever brand.

Need for a change. When things seem to be going well in an organization despite storm clouds ahead, it is hard to create change. Serious problems lead to a search for and acceptance of changing long-term practices and assumptions.

A founder can reflect an organizational heritage and can legitimize an initiative, but there are times in an organization's life when a problem or even a crises stimulates a new or reenergized program. The market threats experienced by the Dove brand, the pressures face by AXE, and the disappointing results of the hand-washing program at Lifebuoy illustrate.

In depth insights. Unilever's brands explored their customer base beyond product experiences to identify real concerns. The result at Dove was the insight that this well-accepted "ideal beauty concept" had such a detrimental effect on women. At Lifebuoy the understanding of the causes of the health issues of kids in developing counties and how to address them drove the "Help a Child Reach 5" program. At AXE, research was conducted and advice solicited from experts revealing the core social pressure on men.

Getting credit. Note how the social programs were linked to the brand. Branding the programs such as "Help a Child Reach 5" and Real Beauty made that link possible or at least stronger. Ben and Jerry's antics provided energy and visibility that was connected to their business and gave them a positive lift among their core community.

Being agile. Be ready to move fast. Issues accelerate, challenges change, and new ones emerge. Programs need to evolve. New partners emerge. The targets need changing. It is often more dynamic than anticipated so "what if" questions need to be on the table

The Challenge is Difficult and Complex

The difficulty of actually creating or finding a societal impact programs and successfully introducing and manage it is both difficult and complex.

Consumers resist change. Unilever found that getting consumers to change was much harder than anticipated. The societal issue for consumers is only one consideration and not necessary as important as others. As a result, the communication of what change is needed, why it will benefit them should be clear and consistent. The need to resist complacency should be part of the process.[23]

Array of needs and programs. Involve a breathtakingly wide scope of societal needs and programs driven in part by a wide array of products, markets, and stakeholders. A variety of approaches is employed to deal with this scope.

Brand family. There were many brands involved in just this version of the Unilever story--Unilever, USLP, Clean Future, Dove, Real Beauty, the Dove Self-Esteem Program, AXE, Lifebuoy, H is for Handwashing, and many more. The role of each of these brands and their ability to provide sometimes critical enhancement to their fellow brand family members needs to be understood and managed.

Influence the system. An individual company can change how it operates but it can't change the system. There is a lot of factors and forces that affect the availability of clean water and the self-esteem of teens is also complex. Even effective programs will rarely be the whole solution.

Partners. It was not a go-it-alone effort but, rather, partners were joined to leverage the Unilever efforts and to make programs more impactful. All these brands had powerful partners that helped make the program effective and scalable.

Measurement is difficult. The measures need to be tailored to the societal need or to the program and to its goals. But relevant measures are difficult to create and in the absence of well-designed experiments, might be ambiguous.

Communicating the Effort—The Role of Signature Brands

What are the signature brands that will carry the flag, will represent the organization or will support other brands? Clearly such brands have a key role and that role will depend on the target audience.

The total organization. The brand Unilever brand and the Unilever Compass (or USLP) brands act as umbrella bands and capture the total social commitment of the firm. This becomes important for employees, investors, suppliers, and other stakeholders. These umbrella brands employ signature brands like the business brands such as Lifebuoy, Dove, and Ben & Jerry's. A notable signature social brand represent the environmental program was "Clean Future" which included a 2030 goal. Environmental efforts too often lack signature brands.

The business brands have their own signature brands. Lifebuoy has "Help a Child Reach 5" and perhaps others. Dove has Real Beauty and the Dove Self-Esteem Program that affect all stakeholders but especially customers. Ben and Jerry's have the founder brands with the colorful heritage of public stunts and strong positions on controversial issues.

The social program brands such as "Help a Child Reach 5" have their own signature brands such as the School of Five and Heroes for Change" that can be important for all stakeholders but particularly for active volunteers and donors.

We now turn to a very different role model, Salesforce.

Chapter 3

SALESFORCE: A SOCIAL PROGRAM PIONEER[24]

Profit in a company is like oxygen for a person. It you don't have enough of it you are out of the game, but if you think your life is about breathing, you are missing something.

Peter Drucker, Business Strategy Guru

Salesforce—Story of Marc Benioff's Vision

Marc Benioff was in his mid-thirties and one of the top executives at fast-growing Oracle when he wanted time to reassess and find meaning in his life beyond superficial business success measures. He decided to take a sabbatical that involved a move to Hawaii and ultimately, a decision to spend two months in India. Inspired by the Indian spiritual leader Mata Amritanandamayi (called the "hugging saint" because she warmly embraces all she meets), he became convinced that doing business and doing good need not be a choice. It was possible to do both, to have a public-service mission built into a firm's purpose and strategy.

When he returned home, he helped start Oracle's Promise, an initiative designed to provide networked computers to disadvantaged schools. It was

49

modeled after General Colin Powell's America's Promise, which fostered a greater commitment among the nation's youth to doing good. In one project, when few employees showed up as planned to help wire a school, Benioff realized a real commitment from businesses and their employees is needed for a social effort to be effective over time.

In 1999, he decided to break away from Oracle and start Salesforce to introduce "software as a service," or cloud computing. This b-to-b service software focused on customer relationship management (CRM), a major enterprise software application. CRM software helps firms manage all elements of the customer experience, including the campaigns to create brand visibility and interest, the resulting customer leads, the buying experience, customer support, customer communities, and customer service.

The big idea was to have Salesforce software reside not in a firm's computers, but on the Internet or "cloud." Because the software is rented instead of bought, there is little upfront investment required, and the expensive installation and maintenance tasks are rather painless, efficient, and out-of-sight. Importantly, software upgrades are installed as they emerge without a disruptive and expensive annual or bi-annual system upgrade or the discomfort of operating software that is not up to date.

Salesforce had obstacles to overcome to persuade firms to risk the new software modality--cloud computing. It had to create software that would be easy to use with a straightforward interface, scalable so that millions could use it, and at the same time, reliable and secure enough to overcome a client's fear of losing control of mission-critical software. These formidable tasks were accomplished by creating software that was fast, simple, right the first time, and fast (worth mentioning twice); by relying on Oracle's database platform and Sun's Java language, both established brands; and by redundancies and programs to enhance reliability.

Addressing the challenge of convincing customers to embrace cloud computing, Salesforce, adopted the persona of a feisty underdog introducing something new and modern in the face of "establishment" firms such as Siebel Systems (a direct competitor) clinging to the past. The firm found novel ways to dramatize the contrast between new and old. During a huge Siebel Users

Group conference at the Moscone Center in San Francisco in February of 2000, Salesforce hired people to picket the hall with signs reading "No Software" and "Software is obsolete." Fake TV reporters provided more hype. An ad showed the contrast between a vintage bi-plane (Siebel) and a modern fighter jet (Salesforce). All got press coverage and social media boosts.

Salesforce was a winner and the exemplar of cloud computing from the outset. A December 1999 article in the Wall Street Journal was entitled "Salesforce Takes the Lead in Latest Software Revolution." Salesforce, also a thought leader, made every effort to be perceived as an industry leader to stay in the forefront. They held "launch events" every six to eight weeks to introduce something new. After one decade, the firm attracted over 65,000 customers and had sales exceeding $1 billion.

Salesforce's mission was to use its CRM software to bring customers and companies together in a new way. In doing so, an important capability was ongoing innovation. One example is the artificial intelligence technology, Salesforce Einstein, which in 2020 was generating more than 1 billion predictions a day. Another is the Salesforce Trailblazer brand community, where customers, partners, and potential customers can have a trusted environment to get answers, share ideas, collaborate, and learn best practices. Then there is their user event, Dreamforce, launched in 2003 with an innovation focus that became an energy force for the brand with over 100,000 attendees, celebrity speakers, and the chance for Salesforce devotees to bond. The second decade saw continued growth. By 2021, sales were over $21 billion, and the firm had a market cap of over $200 billion.

The 1-1-1 (Now Pledge 1%) Corporate Giving Model

Even as the Salesforce got started in one-room apartment with a handful of people in early 1999, Benioff ensured that organizational commitment to societal programs were built into the for-profit business model. To find role models, he looked at firms with effective social/environmental programs.

Taking the best of what he learned, he developed his 1-1-1 system: The organization gave toward social efforts:

- 1 percent of employees' time annually

- 1 percent of its product annually
- 1 percent of its equity

The 1-1-1 brand itself reflects the commitment of Salesforce to a serious societal investment effort. It is also an umbrella brand that gives a host of social programs a home, rationale, and credibility. And a signature brand because it represents the societal efforts of Salesforce. Other firms were challenged to accept the 1-1-1 model. Because for some of them, 1% of equity was not workable, 1% of the profits was added as an alternative commitment. The revised version of the program also got a name change to Pledge 1%.

By 2022, over 15,000 firms representing over 100 countries had taken the pledge. The Pledge 1% idea and brand had spread, and with it, the Salesforce brand and influence.

These firms that have accepted the Salesforce challenge can use the visibility of the Pledge 1% brand to provide credibility to their firm's efforts to address society's problems and needs. The Pledge 1% brand itself communicates what it is, a commitment to use meaningful level corporate resources to do societal good. The value of the Pledge 1% brand comes from its heritage, as dramatically told by the signature story of Marc Benioff's early days of founding Salesforce. For many of the firms, that story has given both inspiration and motivation.

For Salesforce and many other firms, the Pledge 1% represents the minimum investment each year; often, much more is delivered. The Salesforce employees, on average, actually volunteered substantially more than the 1% target, which would be 2 days a year. In fiscal 2021, the value of its donated and discounted technology, grants, and volunteerism was estimated to be over 1.5 billion, which is over 6% of sales and more than 100% of net income, clearly exceeding the commitment goals.

Marc Benioff is an important personal brand with respect to building and evolving the software as a service (cloud) subcategory, and with respect to his leadership in the concept of a business that elevates all stakeholders, particularly the community, society, and the planet. Among his observations:

- "Companies can do more than just make money, they can serve others. The business of business, is improving the state of the world." [25]

- "The real joy in life comes from giving. It comes from service. It comes from doing things for other people."[26]

Benioff buttresses his stature and credibility, with respect to having a social mission for business, by his personal interest in community problems. He has supported efforts to deal with the homeless, for example, and has challenged others to do the same. He and his wife have given major gifts to create the UCSF Benioff Children's Hospitals, a world-class safety-net hospital that serves all children, regardless of financial or immigration status. Over half the patients are covered by Medi-Cal, health insurance for low-income households. The result is that the Benioff brand plays a key role in the Salesforce societal effort, giving it visibility, credibility, and distinctiveness with respect to efforts lift society, to enhance what Salesforce calls "people and the planet."

Salesforce with 1-1-1, now Pledge 1%, as the cornerstone, has engaged in two decades of social programs and community activism that has remarkable depth, breadth, and impact. During that time, it has participated with dozens of globally influential organizations such as the Social Sustainability Committee of the Consumer Goods Forum, which drives global collaboration between retailers and manufacturers while identifying and tackling key societal issues, such as eradicating forced labor. Another is the World Economic Forum (WEF) Global Future Council: The Future of Human Rights, which aims to better understand the potential impact of the fourth industrial revolution on human rights.

The Salesforce social program success record has resulted in a stream of awards, including placing number 6 in Fortune's Best Workplaces in 2020, the 13th consecutive year it has made the list. It often places near the top and is regularly named as one of Fortune's top ten Most Admired Companies in the World. It was named as Forbes Innovator of the Decade in 2017, the number 2 firm in Barron's Most Sustainable Companies List in 2018, and number 1 or 2 from 2015 to 2020 on the on the Companies that Care list created by People magazine, and based on large scale employee interviews. In a b-to-b space that Salesforce resides, such awards bolster an already firm position as a leader in the "make profit while doing good" space.

The effort to address society's challenges is coordinated by the Salesforce Foundation (salesforce.org) organization and is distinct from the Salesforce business. At the same time, they are interconnected and overlapping because many of the social programs, such as those involving software or volunteers, are embedded in the core Salesforce organization. The foundation aims to make the world a better place with the most meaningful, measurable, sustainable change possible for individuals and communities around the world.[27]

To understand the scope and impact of the Salesforce.com societal effort, we look at the major thrusts of the Pledge 1% program—Technology for Social Change, Workforce Development, Citizen Philanthropists, and Environmental initiatives.

Technology for Social Change

Salesforce believes technology can make a difference and also enhance and accelerate social program impact. The goal is to empower changemakers in nonprofits who are focused on societal problems, education, philanthropy, the environment to build a better world by providing access to powerful Salesforce technology. The umbrella brand, Technology for Social Change, takes on a signature status at least for some audiences.

The **"Power of Us"** program is the Salesforce vehicle to provide free or discounted Salesforce technology plus success training and resources to nonprofit organizations so that they can be more effective and, in some cases, be able to operate at all. Since the firm's founding, the Power of Us program has provided all eligible organizations 10 free Salesforce licenses, industry data models, and discounted products. In 2021, Salesforce.org donated technology and pro bono support worth more than $1.5 billion through the Power of Us program.

There are a core set of software suites that help nonprofits, who have overwhelming challenges, with keeping track of relationships with clients, client alumni, volunteers, staff members, donors, and prospective donors, plus managing a tracking system for program-related work and linking with an employee help center, a client information system, a client community and more. One Salesforce platform is the **Nonprofit Success Pack**, which supports databases across volunteers, donors, and clients; helps manage the interactions and relationship with all three groups; and provides industry reports and a dashboard that allows performance to be monitored. Another is the **Nonprofit**

Cloud, which supports fundraising by creating donor-centric experiences, engaging supporters, and simplifying and integrating grantmaking. Salesforce programs helped Big Brothers Big Sisters of America (BBBS) deal with the complex and sensitive issue of screening and matching volunteers to "littles" with messaging and databases in a secure environment. It also helps the ability of BBBS mentor training to access its resource library. The **Marketing Cloud for Nonprofits** helps them with the marketing challenges.

Another vehicle, the **Education Cloud**, is directed toward nonprofit educational organizations. Colleges need to find, engage, and enroll the best-fit students, deliver services, drive retention for those students, and then build the ongoing alumni and donor relationship. Not easy, and software can make a huge difference.

Still another is the **Philanthropy Cloud**, connecting companies and their employees globally with the causes they are most passionate about. It helps firms and people keep track of their giving and provides indicators of its impact. A fourth is the **Sustainability Cloud,** used to quickly track and analyze environmental data to help firms move toward a carbon emissions reduction goal.

The pandemic created a **Salesforce Care for Employee and Customer Support** software application for organizational life for nonprofits in the pandemic. A pre-configured employee help center, customer service, and contact center application for responding to inquiries fast and keep customers and employees informed.

One Salesforce customer, Teach for America, addresses the fact that more than 16 million children in the United States live in poverty without access to a quality education, by recruiting and developing recent college graduates to teach in needy communities and become lifelong leaders in addressing educational inequity. Teach For America now fields a corps of 11,000 teachers, has an alumni network of more than 32,000 and 2,500 employees across 48 regions nationwide. Coordination between these three groups and prospective teachers and school districts is messy and Salesforce software can help. The Salesforce1 Mobile App, for example, lets recruiters easily connect with prospects to join Teach for America in the field anytime and anywhere, eliminating lag time from the process. It also provides links to the social media world, which helps them understand and drive conversations in the education space.

Workforce Development—Improving Access to Education

The battle against inequality depends on elevating the capability of those not sharing in the fruits of technology. They may have lacked access to or motivation for the relevant education. Or their expertise was no longer needed because of a technological advance. This effort not only addressees education inequality but also society's challenge of creating a future work force that is relevant to the digital age. In 2019, Benioff signed the White House Pledge, committing to provide training to 1 million Americans.

One workforce development tactic is to help the disadvantaged K-12 schools, starting with Oakland and San Francisco (which are in its "backyard"), and then extending to other major cities. The strategy is to recognize and support organizations, through grants and employee volunteer effort, that have been making progress with effective programs to help students in elementary and secondary schools with motivation, as well as academics. They are seeing progress. The number of students taking computer classes and the number of middle-school students proficient in math are both rising substantially in target schools.

Another tactic supports and mentors organization that assisting students who have little family support in getting into college. Recognizing that student progress also involves basics such as stable food and housing, supporting organizations who address that challenge has become part of the program. Salesforce also provides intern employment for these students in a **"Future Force Program."**

A third effort is to support training to supply in-demand skills for those that need jobs or better jobs. The signature effort is based on Salesforce's own training program designed to create Trailblazers, people who are credentialed to operate in Salesforce software ecosystem. It is available not only to Salesforce employees, but to anyone that would like to create the capability to participate in the greater Salesforce ecosystem. There are hundreds of courses centrally located on the Trailhead website that run from 2 to 18 hours, are free, and include topics like "Get started with Salesforce Cloud" or "Managing volunteers for nonprofits." They not only lead to job-relevant knowledge, but also provide resume-building credentials.

Trailhead's mission is to reduce the barriers to learning and provide anyone, regardless of their background or education level, with the tools needed to land a job in the thriving Salesforce ecosystem. If you are a job seeker looking to skill up for the future and transform your own career, Trailhead empowers you to succeed in today's new normal. Trailblazer thus acts as a business brand and a social brand.

People can also join the Trailblazer community to receive help in learning the software, finding mentors, and even landing a job. Jesse Twum-Boato was stymied in his job until he took ten certificated Salesforce courses at Trailhead and became a solutions architect for PwC in South Africa, a career that seemed implausible before Trailhead changed his resume.[28] The Salesforce **Pathfinder**, initiated in 2017, formalized a set of these courses into a coherent curriculum geared to elevate the Trailhead experience.

Salesforce is also looking to their own employees to make sure they are motivated to keep up with their field and be prepared for the evolution occurring in their workplace, and capable of advancing at Salesforce and achieving their potential. For example, **Leading Ohana** (Hawaiian for "family") is a full-year program designed to elevate future leaders into mindful, socially aware, globally oriented leaders that will take the business to the next level. All have the opportunity to work with an organization in developing communities.

Citizen Philanthropists

The idea is to let each employee select a societal need that he or she believes would benefit from a volunteer or grant. It is social entrepreneurship at the most basic level relying on person close to the need experience. The umbrella brand, Citizen Philanthropists, provides a way to communicate this effort content such as stories, the number of hours spent, and impact measures.

A prime way to make a difference is by volunteering. In 2021, 72% of employees did volunteer. Whether to provide a lesson to a third-grade class, council a college applicant, be on the board of a food bank, or help a nonprofit organization fundraise, volunteering creates intimacy and involvement that can be satisfying and effective. This volunteer work could also leverage professional skills and even Salesforce software to have more impact.

One such volunteer from Salesforce-Ireland became attached to St. Marin's school, located in the heart of a slum in Nairobi, Kenya, a 250-person high school with an adjacent 500-person primary school.[29] A dozen or so Salesforce people were attracted and made a difference with donations, equipment, and consulting. A group went to Africa and met nine former students that had graduated from college, an achievement that, given the background, was astounding. There was a lot of dancing, planning, celebrating, and pride.

Donating is a way to make employees feel and act as citizen philanthropists. Their ability to find causes and programs that merit support can be leveraged. Salesforce matches up to $5,000 per employee per year to support causes that our employees care about. This empowers employees to become citizen philanthropists.

Environmental Efforts

Early in the life of Salesforce, at an annual company open forum, a customer support analyst, Sue Amor, asked what Salesforce was doing about the environment. Benioff replied by asking her to take six paid days off to figure it out. That challenge would become a turning point in her career and an impetus for what became a major priority for the firm. She came back with a plan for the firm to reduce its carbon footprint. She later helped form and lead the "**Earth Council,**" an employee-run group that examined grass-roots changes within the company to address the climate crisis. But the story didn't end there. In its next phase, she was assigned to a new role as the first sustainability manager at Salesforce, helping it establish an environmental mission statement and integrate policies supporting sustainable business practices.

The result was a multipronged approach. One initiative was to join a coalition of business, civil society, and UN leaders to set 1.5-degree science-based emission reduction targets. Part of this tactic was to reduce the emissions from suppliers and from the use of fuel by employees while traveling. Still, another was to use 100% renewable energy within a few years as part of the effort is make the cloud carbon-neutral. Others come from supporting nonprofits that were engaged in energy-reducing programs, such as "Cool Effect", that replaces wood-burning stoves with more fuel-efficient ones and uses Salesforce technology to manage photos of households using the to make sure the stoves are working. Then there was the Trillion Tree program and the Sustainability cloud platforms.

Salesforce committed to conserving or restoring 100 million trees by 2030 as part of the Trillion Tree effort launched in 2020 at the World Economic Forum to mobilize the global movement to put 1 trillion new or restored trees on the ground by 2030, because rebuilding forest is a crucial part of reducing global warming and biodiversity collapse. The effort, for which Salesforce is a sponsor and Marc and Lynne Benioff are major donors, is guided by evidence about the degradation of forests and its effect and studies of forest building programs that work.

Another initiative was to mobilize software assets via the **Salesforce Sustainability Cloud**, which allows businesses to gain true visibility into their environmental data, including carbon emissions. A company's historical and real-time carbon footprint data can be visualized in dynamic reports and dashboards—both for audit purposes and for executive engagement. Companies can even track direct and indirect emissions from their entire value chain. To support, there is the **Carbon Account Playbook** guide to understanding carbon accounting, the environmental footprint, and what action is needed.

Commitment to Measurement

At Salesforce, what gets measured gets done. Within Salesforce, a dedicated team uses data and evidence whenever and wherever possible. It comes in three forms.

First, research and analysis help reveal where problems are acute and where Salesforce assets and knowledge can play a role in making meaningful change. That leads to the task of improving education and the effectiveness of nonprofits. For example, the Salesforce Nonprofit Trends Report shows how digital maturity contributes to adaptive strategies, supporter acquisition, and program innovation within nonprofits.

Second, Salesforce societal investments in money, people, and programs are monitored to ensure that the effort is substantial, the priorities are correct, and creative change and improvement are being built in. The effort is contrasted with the past to ensure that there is positive vitality and adaptability.

Third, and most importantly, there is a focus on outcomes as well as inputs because the goal is not to expend resources, but to change and impact.[30] The search is consequently for evidence that programs are delivering meaningful, measurable, and sustainable change across the primary portfolios. Outcome measurement is difficult and frustrating because the data is often not easily available and there can be second-order effects that are material, yet too easily ignored. In 2019, the outcome measures at Salesforce were estimated to have a value of over $1.1 billion.

Reflections

Even though the two firms are very different, one is a b-to-b (business to business) corporate brand, and the other is a b-to-c (business to consumer) family of brands, it is remarkable how similar the strategies and challenges seem in the two stories.

Salesforce, like Unilever, effectively integrated their business strategy and supporting culture with their social programs effort. The heritage umbrella program Pledge 1% (formerly 1-1-1) provided substance to the commitment of the firm to doing social good and its leadership in this arena. The CEO, Marc Benioff, provided energy and credibility to the Salesforce societal programs. Many impactful signature social programs where embedded or next to the business software and supporting programs such as Trailblazer, Trailhead, Pathfinder, and the cloud brands, which is the ultimate level of integration.

Salesforce shared with Unilever the use of partners, strategic agility, and gaining in-depth insights into the societal problems they addressed. At Salesforce, that insight generally came by applying their products in an arena of societal need. Both found the challenge of creating and communicating a social effort challenging because of the wide array of societal needs and responsive programs involved, the realization that any program is embedded in a larger system, the challenge of finding and working with partners, and difficult measurement issues.

A big difference, of course, is that the Salesforce brand is a master brand that drives the products and societal programs, while Unilever is a corporate brand that endorses over a hundred major business brands such as Lifebuoy or Dove. The Salesforce brand, thus, needs to wear two hats, a business/product brand and a social hat. Having two hats risks the societal role receiving inadequate internal and external attention, a risk that did not surface at Salesforce. Salesforce, because of its master brand status, likely causes more of the societal effort to come from the bottom up, from employees, customers, and nonprofit organizations in need.

Continuing to provide a context for the "future of purpose-driven branding" discussion, we look at the forces driving firms and their stakeholders to build an effective effort to address society's challenges.

Chapter 4

FIVE DRIVERS OF SOCIAL EFFORT MOMENTUM

*At this moment in history, and from this point forward,
companies will be judged by more than the profits they generate.
They will be measured by the value they created for society.*
Enrique Lores, President and CEO, HP

C reating social (or societal) purpose or mission and programs has changed from "nice to do" to "must do" for a surging number of firms. Most firms have, or are considering getting, a societal effort in place. The question has turned from "should we" to "how can we" find or create social programs that can be well-executed and create a difference-making impact. There is momentum, but still a large gap between the current social effort of the private sector and the potential impact that is possible and is coming.

Societal programs, of course, have been in place for well over a century. Recall in Chapter 2 the image of William Hesketh Lever in 1894, founding what is now Unilever because of a desire to preserve health, by fighting cholera, through better hygiene? There were others. Milton Hershey, who by trial and error discovered a way to make chocolate bars, built his first factory in 1903 in the town that now bears his name and he acted very different from the industrialist of his day. He built homes, parks, schools, and infrastructure that enriched his employees, and built and endowed a school for orphaned boys. He was not about maximizing profits. Both Lever and Hershey were the oddballs of commerce in those days.

In the midcentury, the concept of a business having programs that helped society started to advance. In 1954, Peter Drucker, the management guru of the time, wrote that a major task of executives is to manage the social responsibility of business, in part, because business exists for the sake of society.[31] But still, the private sector was largely focused on ad hoc philanthropic grants. Few firms were making impact with focused, goal-directed, competently run societal programs, programs that address society challenges such as climate change, resource depletion, inequality, health, and education.

The drive toward social programs in business kept rising through the decades. It was captured by the CSR (corporate social responsibility) concept, originally coined in 1953 by the economist, Howard Bowen, in his book Social Responsibilities of the Businessman. CSR focuses on running a business fairly and honesty and improving the community and environment in which it operates.

In 1987 the Sustainability label appeared, the idea that business activities today should not compromise future generations. The term is used by some to represent environmental issues such as climate change and resource depletion, but, in most contexts, is broader and includes challenges relating to education, health, and inequality.

In 2005, the ESG (environment, social, governance) concept was developed to guide investors that would like to have portfolios of companies that demonstrate good behavior with respect to the three dimensions and avoiding bad behavior. It appeared in a report entitled "Who Cares Wins" that was sponsored by a joint initiative of 50 financial CEOs organized at the behest of UN secretary general Kofi Annan. As noted in Chapter 1, efforts to measure ESG has limitations—they do not measure social performance of business units within firms, their ability to measure what they claim to measure has been questioned, and the hundreds of dimensions they consider tends to overwhelm any effort to recognize and reward programs with real impact on societal challenges. Nevertheless, it is an indicator of the interest among investors that firms take seriously their involvement in societal problems and needs.

One indicator of the ascent of social programs in business is the use of long, detailed annual firm impact reports which include quantitative goals and progress reports about their role in addressing society problems and issues. In 2020, over 90 percent of Fortune 500 firms filed such a report, a big step up from 2012 when 20% were filed.[32] This reporting effort is global and not just for the largest firms--the 2020 KPMG survey found that 80 percent of the largest 100 firms in 52 countries, 5200 companies in total, filed a report on the performance of their societal efforts.[33] Another indicator—alterations in corporate structure. In 2021, for example, 47 percent of S&P 500 firms had a chief diversity officer, two-thirds of whom had been appointed in the prior three years.[34] The presence of a chief sustainability officer is now even more common.

Figure 4-1

FIVE DRIVERS OF SOCIAL PURPOSE AND PROGRAMS

Stakeholder Paradigm is Winning

Visible Societal Challenges

Businesses Have Resources and Agility to Contribute

Social Purpose and Programs as a Priority

Employees and Other Stakeholders Demand it

Business Brand Gets Energy and Image Lift

Five drives of this momentum shown in Figure 4-1 are in evidence and provide a context for what is facing firms.

The Stakeholder Paradigm Is Winning.

There has been a lengthy and intense fight for the soul of capitalization between whether an enterprise should only "maximize shareholder return" or whether it should serve all stakeholders including the employees, the community, society at large, and the planet. When the shareholder model has traction, those promoting societal programs face an internal head wind.

The shareholder model has its intellectual roots in the world of Austrian economists such as Frederich Hayek, who won a Nobel Prize in 1974, whose writings in the mid-twentieth century, in part reacting to European socialism, argued that a free market unencumbered by excess regulation and "safety nets" was the best system to address society's needs.

This free market concept was famously institutionalized by the Chicago economist, Milton Freeman, who in a 1970 *New York Times* essay declared that—"there is one and only one social responsibility of business—to increase its profits." Reinforced by Adam's elegant "invisible hand" which posits that optimal pricing and efficient production will follow when all market participants engage in profit maximization. The shareholder model hypothesizes that more profits fund new innovation that can improve products, ensure the health and survival of the firm, and provide tax revenue for social services.

The elevation of stock return as the primary business objective was reinforced by an important article in 1976 in which, two economists, Michael Jensen and William Meckling, argued that maximizing profits should be goal of a business and any other activity such as charitable giving or excess employee benefits would only distract.[35] Further, they argued that executives should receive stock or stock options to insure that they have an incentive to deliver shareholder return. This idea got traction and not only supported the shareholder model but contributed to the a surge in the growth in wage inequality.

The theory behind the shareholder model got a huge boost when Jack Welch started his two decade long CEO role at GE in 1981 as David Gelles documented in his book, "The Man that Broke Capitalism."[36] Welsh took a firm with a respected reputation for innovation and concern for employees and their communities and spent his tenure with a fixation on increasing profits and stock price.

Welch was ruthless in the pursuit of profits. He made employees expendable as he engaged in radical downsizing (he believed in firing the bottom 10% each year), outsourcing (chasing bargains), offshoring (one solution to obstinate unions), and selling off business units (fix it, close it, or sell it was one of his dictums) all to improve the bottom line. Instead of investing in strategic R&D, the GE heritage, he engaged in stock buy-backs and acquisitions designed to improve short-term profits. He aggressively encouraged the GE finance business, GE Capital, to engage in risky loans and insurance bets that provided a major ongoing profit lift (accounting for 60% of profits at one point), Not a brand builder, his only corporate advertising was on the financial networks. When his business was found to be a dangerous polluter he avoided responsibility. And do-gooder programs did not pass the profit screen.

Success and admiration came to Welch. Under his leadership, GE's market value went from $14 billion to $600 billion representing a 21% return per year and, not incidentally, he became a billionaire, an executive guru, and revered role model. He was named by Fortune as the executive of the century and Businessweek declared him the "gold standard against which other CEOs are measured." He made the shareholder model healthy and even envied. When he left GE in 2001, the shareholder model may have reached its high point.

We now know that the Welch success came at a huge cost to employees, communities, the country, the planet, and ultimately to GE itself, which during succeeding years lost 80% of its stock value and required a $140 million government bailout in 2009 just to stay in business. There were also GE influenced spillover effects during the Welch years such as a decrease in factory employment and the increase in earnings disparity. The percent of the before tax income earned by the top 1%, for example, essentially doubled from 1980 to 2000, from 10% to 20%.[37] And the average compensation of CEOs of the top US companies rose from $1.85 million in 1980 to 21.5 million in 2000.[38]

The Welch reputation and that of the shareholder model suffered after he left, although the fall did not get the same press as the rise. Further, eight or so of the Welch trained top GE executives were hired to run major firms. Although the results of two of the firms was ambiguous, in at least six of them including Boeing, Albertson, and Home Depot, the focus on shareholder returns led to disastrous results.[39] It became clear that policies that Welch made not only acceptable but admired, are destructive on many levels.

Enter the stakeholder model which argues that multiple stakeholders deserve to be served by a capitalistic business firm in addition to shareholders. Each of these represent an important pillar of organizational long-term vitality and existence. While shareholders provide financial capital, a necessary asset, other stakeholders provide other assets such as human talent, customer loyalty, supplier reliability, a stable and safe society, infrastructure (Internet, roads, rail tracks, living space, utilities, etc.), and resources (energy, water, metals, air). It seems logical that their role should be acknowledged, and they should receive a return for their contribution. In addition, without business firms attacking societal problems, it is likely that there will be a less livable planet, a scarcity of resources, deterioration of infrastructure, more poverty, social inequality, an unhealthy population, and economic decline that will affect even the most well-managed organization.

News flash! The battle is not over, but the good guys are winning! Those firms that aspire to have empathy, heart, a social purpose or mission, and a solid and effective set of social programs are seeing their ideas carry the day. There are several visible indicators that a winner is emerging even though there are still pockets of resistance and there is a lot of upsides left for those on board.

In 2019, The Business Round Table, who represent the CEOs of America's leading companies, replaced their "shareholder is dominate" purpose statement of 1997 with a new purpose statement that explicitly stated that firms need to deliver value to all the stakeholders, which includes a commitment to protect the environment.[40] Over 180 CEOs of firms representing 30% of the capitalization within the US stock market personally signed onto the new purpose. Alex Gorsky, CEO of Johnson & Johnson and chair of the group, opined that the new statement "affirms the essential role corporations can play in improving our society when CEOs are truly committed to meeting the needs of all stakeholders."[41]

Companies have stepped up to the climate change challenge. A 2021 report from BCG (Boston Consulting Group) and the World Economic Forum based on two dozen CEO interviews, the analysis of industry reports, and multiple data bases reported that 9,000 firms worldwide had reported their carbon emissions and 3,000 of those had set carbon reduction goals, up from 900 in 2017. There was still a long way to go as these companies were still in the minority, but clearly there was momentum.[42]

The continued growth of the "certified b corp," which confers the status of a business that has documented its effort to balance profit with efforts to serve their stakeholders and be a force for good, is relevant. Formed in 2006, 82 firms qualified the next year. The certification process is detailed, distracting, time consuming, and must be repeated every two years. Yet fifteen years later, over 4,000 firms qualified, including Ben & Jerry's and Patagonia.

There are hundreds of books that recount the struggle and provide perspectives on why the stakeholder model needs to prevail. Some helpful books with titles that often summarize the message include:

- Conscious Capitalism: Liberating the Heroic Spirit of Business by John Mackey and Raj Sisodia
- Confronting Capitalism: Real Solutions for a Troubled Economic System by Philip Kotler
- The Purpose Economy: How Your Desire for Impact, Personal Growth, and Community is Changing the World by Aaron Hurst
- Grow the Pie: How Great Companies Deliver Both Purpose and Profit by Alex Edmans
- Net Positive: How Courageous Companies Thrive by Giving More Than They Take by Paul Polman and Andrew Winston

MBA programs are now featuring societal issues and how to manage them, reflecting thought leadership and the interests of students. The Wharton School offers more than 50 undergraduate and graduate courses related to societal impact. At the Harvard Business School, 600 students took a second-year elective course related to social enterprise in 2020, as compared with 250 in 2012.[43]

Then there were the public statements from business leaders. In 2018, in a letter to CEOs, Larry Fink, the head of BlackRock and the world's largest asset manager, wrote "to prosper over time every company must not only deliver financial performance, but also show how it makes a positive contribution the society."[44] He later added "profits are in no way inconsistent with purpose—in fact, profits and purpose are inextricably linked." Two years later, Bill Gates in a speech in Davos, called for a new "creative capitalism", which would feature a business system with a twin mission: making profits and also improving lives for those who don't fully benefit from market forces.

It just feels right to help society with its problems. It feels right to help those that lack access to health services, education, housing, sufficient food, clean water, uncontaminated land, and the riches of a healthy economy. It feels right to give back to a society that provides social order, social well-being, social energy, a healthy planet, and economic health, all of which are important resources and assets on which most firms are built. It feels right to find meaning in work. It feels right to be doing something that your friends, employees, customers, investors respect and admire.

There is still work to be done to solidify the victory. The winners need to not only be supported and rewarded, but also motivated to set higher and broader goals. Others who are slow-walking in their societal efforts, who offer a lot of words but little substance, or develop off-the-mark or ineffective programs need to be encouraged to do better. Those that still don't get it need to be identified and held accountable.

The responsibility for providing ongoing support for the stakeholder model and holding firms accountable goes beyond business executives and their boards. It includes consumers, employees, investors, business school professors, influential writers and more. It will take a village to make sure the soul of business, indeed capitalism, is healthy and has the right priorities.

Where did this momentum come from? The remaining four drivers play a role.

Employees and Other Stakeholders Demand It.

There is pressure for firms to make meaningful progress on societal problems from many fronts. There are governmental agencies, the general public, society advocates, and more. But the most relevant sources of influence are employees, customers, and investors.

Employees Quest for Meaning. Employees need a higher purpose in today's world. Increasing sales and profits and getting a paycheck is not enough to provide adequate answers to the "Why?" question. Employees, including executives, want to respect and admire their firm and want their jobs to have meaning in their professional lives.

A variety of studies have shown that employees motivated by a social mission will be more likely to join a firm, turn their back on opportunities to leave the firm, and work effectively and enthusiastically toward the firm's goals. The Deloitte Insights 2019 global survey covering the US and four other countries found, for example, that purpose-driven companies had 40% higher levels of work force retention than their competitors.[45] The study by BCG and World Economic Forum published in 2021 (already mentioned) estimated that about half of employees believe that sustainability policies affect their decision to stay at their firm, or which firm to join.[46]

The influence of social programs on employees is much higher among millennials. The Cone Communication Millennial Employee study found that 64% of Millennials (born 1980 to 1994) won't take a job if their employee doesn't have a strong CSR policy, and 83% would be more loyal to a company that helps them contribute to social issues (vs. 70% U.S. average).[47] When it comes to Gen-Z (born 1995 to 2015), the newest entry into the workforce, the data is even more compelling.

Customer Preference. There is a substantial group of customers that say that their purchase decisions and brand loyalty is influenced by whether organizations have a social purpose and active, effective social programs. For example, a 2019 survey of 1,000 U.S. adults found that respondents were more likely to have a positive image of (89%), trust in (86%) and loyalty to (83%) brands that lead with purpose and 66% would switch from a product they typically buy from to a purpose-driven company.[48] A purpose company is one assumed to prioritize social programs.

The annual Edelman Trust Barometer, with 20 years history, measures trust and a variety of other dimensions with over 1,000 adult respondents in each of 28 countries. In the 2020 report, they note that brands are expected to solve both societal and personal problems (86 percent), support me (68 percent), and support my community (63 percent).[49]

Amazon conducted, with Environics Research, a global study about how a firm's social values shape buying decisions. Over 80% of U.S. and European consumers think more brands should do their part in helping the world and 55% of U.S. consumers and 70% of European consumers are more likely to buy a brand that is willing to take a stand on social issues.[50]

Of course, behavior in the marketplace does not always mirror these sentiments, but even a small percentage taking action can mean the difference between marginal financial performance and a thriving, growing business. Also, consumer sentiment includes those that will speak out by recommending a brand to others or sharing a commentary over social media, the most influential endorsement possible.

Investors. Investors, at least a solid group of them, have changed sides. They are looking to buy firms that hold the stakeholder view of business. Social Responsible Investing (SRI) has actually been around for half a century or, by some accounts, back since the early days of the United States. At one time, it involved a stock holding boycott of South Africa because of apartheid. Rockefeller foundation coined the term "impact investing" in 2007 where portfolios would focus on societal goals plus ROI. Where SRI is sometimes seen as focusing on screening out sin stocks. "Impact investing" emphasizes the firm's intentional creation of positive impact.

A result of the 2004 Kofi Annon initiative mentioned above, an organization called Principles for Responsible Investing (PRI) was formed with a mission that included a commitment to incorporate societal issues into investment decisions and stock ownership policies. PRI, which started with approximately 100 financial entities, had grown by 2021 to over 4,000 signatories who represented over a $120 trillion in AUM (assets under management).[51]

A key question is: what kind of financial performance can be expected from impact investing? The GIIN organization (Global Impact Investing Network) has some answers.[52] GIIN is a large global community of impact investors and service providers that provide infrastructure, support activities, education, and research for members.

GIIN's research shows that about one third of impact investors accept below-market rate returns to achieve strategic objectives and two-thirds aspire to achieve market rate or better returns. In total, 20% exceed their financial goals and 12% fall short. With respect to impact goals, 21% are exceeded and only 1% fall short.[53] Second, an analysis of the many impact investing studies in the field yields some observations. There is a wide dispersion of financial performance, of impact investing funds depending on the nature of the portfolio composition, the societal needs involved, and the quality of the fund management. On average, an impact investor can deliver as good as or better financial performance as a non-impact investor. Across various strategies and asset classes, top quartile impact investor funds seeking market-rate returns perform at similar levels to peers using conventional investment strategies. In many cases, median performance is also quite similar. ·

There is a segment of the investor community, however, that looks to take over firms and instill a squeeze strategy—ruthlessly reducing headcount, strategic investments in brands, and offering improvements through R&D in order to improve short-term margins, profits, and most important, per-share earnings. An entity specializing in that strategy attempted to buy Unilever in 2017 with an eye to quickly cut the "unnecessary" expenditures which would surely have crippled the Unilever extensive social efforts. This group was fought off with a PR sprint, marshaling logic and data to sympathetic investors and government agencies. The lesson is that the "good" investors need to be attracted, the strategic story should be compelling and at the ready, and the social programs should enhance the business so that killing them off is not an easy way to increase short-term cash flow.

The Seriousness and Visibility of Societal Problems

Throughout history, an increase in the visibility of societal problems has precipitated action from government and from business. In the 60s, for example, the books Silent Spring by Rachel Carson on the fallout from pesticides, Ralph Nader's "Unsafe at any Speed," and The Feminine Mystique by Betty Friedan called attention to problems facing society that precipitated change.[54] In the same time frame, we had a movement labeled consumerism with Jack Kennedy's rights of consumers as a flag bearer that precipitated a host of programs by businesses.

The Santa Barbara oil spill in early 1969, then the largest oil spill in the United States waters, created energy for the emerging environmental movement. One result was the first annual Earth Day held April 22, 1970, when 20 million people took to the streets across the United States to protest environmental destruction.

The visibility of societal problems represented by trends, events, and stories has been ongoing, but in the last two decades they have gotten more frequent, intense, compelling, and frightening. Each is being magnified by the social media and cable news world. In addition, a variety of organizations have elevated the discussion with greater knowledge of the causes and evolution of the problems, operational measures, and visibility. For example, the United Nations in 2015created a set of Sustainable Goals that were adopted by over 190 countries. The 17 goal categories, such as eliminating hunger and poverty, are detailed and measurable and many firms link their social efforts to whichever of these goals are relevant.

We will now focus on four major society problems—climate change, inequality, health, and education, with a comment that problems facing people in poor countries are greatly magnified and the governments with a primary responsibility to address these and other problems have limitations and need help and support. The most visible and influential of these has been climate change and how its impact has propelled the total stakeholder movement.

Climate change. Climate change is directly, or indirectly, creating very visible droughts, heat waves, fires, severe weather events, rising sea levels, oceans that are warming and becoming more acidic, the death of animal species and more. People have heard for over a half-century about climate change, the dramatic increase in CO_2 in the atmosphere, its causes, and possible solutions. But in the last decade, its visible effects have become so dramatic, so extreme, and so measurable that a realistic glimpse of the future becomes possible.

The 2021 UN climate report from over 230 scientists is sobering, if not terrifying. It affirms that the climate change is man-made from sources such as fossil fuel burning and deforestation and will continue putting agriculture, fishing, and even living a "normal" lifestyle at risk.[55] António Guterres, the UN's secretary-general, described the situation in simpler (and scarier) terms as a "code red for humanity"[56]

The adverse impact of climate change is increasingly apparent and has, or will soon adversely affect the short-term economic health of many firms. It is not just a future possibility. The accessibility of power and water for farms and homes, for example, is affected by climate change. The food companies' ability to rely on agriculture is also at risk because projected increases in temperatures, changes in precipitation patterns, changes in extreme weather events, and reductions in water availability will result in reduced agricultural productivity.

Inequality. Inequality of wealth and income is, by most measures, getting worse decade by decade which means that many are living on the edge or worse. The lack of access to food and housing for many has become more apparent with stretched food banks and increased homeless presence. The lack of employment opportunities in a world in which automation and artificial intelligence is threatening jobs from retail clerks to drivers of trucks and delivery vans, is more obvious. The unequal treatment under the law based on racial and ethnic backgrounds, in part voiced by the Black Lives Matter movement, touched many.

Health. There is a pervasive set of health issues that are increasingly visible. There is the impact of diets that include the intake of sugar, fat, salt, and additives in food that are mostly supplied by private firms and the related risks of being overweight, especially among the young. Another problem is a sedentary population segment where video games have replaced active exercise. A more general problem is that the medical system in the US is excessively costly and provides, by many measures, inadequate access to major segments of society.

Education. The inadequate education opportunities from kindergarten to college is a reality for a large and growing segment of the population and is one of the root causes of the increase in inequality. Out of an average 21-person class in middle and high school, fewer than 13 will pursue college work, increasingly a requirement of jobs in the digital age. That number falls to just over 7 for black Americans.[57] Too often, high schools lack resources, a wide scope of courses, and motivated students. The problem goes back to primary and middle schools where the motivation for college is not fostered or supported. The US is low on social mobility, 26 countries are ranked higher, in part because access to quality, or even adequate, education is limited for many. Helping the education system is a fruitful area for social programs for many firms.

Low-income countries. These problems are all much more acute in low-income counties that struggle with poverty and unreliable or unavailable necessities such as power, internet access, and public safety. Images of kids without food, clean water, access to education are visible on global media, often graphically. The fact that such populations have little economic power means that the task of coupling social programs with business enhancement is more challenging.

Government's Limitations. It is becoming clear that the governments of the world, while a critical part of the solution, are not able to cope by themselves with these societal problems. There is political gridlock and decision paralysis through much of the world. Further, government debt levels reduce the ability to fund programs. Finally, governmental societal programs struggle with their often plodding "one size fits all" solutions to address societal problems that have a local face and require agle adaptive strategies. Governments need help.

Businesses with Resources, Insights, and Agility Can Contribute

Since the 1890s when Unilever founder William Hesketh Lever set out to preserve health through better hygiene, the bulk of societal efforts by business firms, as noted above, consisted of ad hoc philanthropy grants with the amount of grant expenditures as the measuring stick of impact. Over the last half century, a more professional approach into managing social programs, both within firms and at nonprofits, has gradually emerged. This has instilled confidence that it can be done, and that competence is actually the norm. It also counters the argument that such programs should not be a priority because amateurs, sometime volunteers, will be running the show, resulting in ineffective and inefficient results.

In comparison to a government entity, a business firm has assets to bring to the party. In particular, business firms have:

- **Management competence.** Inherent ability and experience in managing strategically and tactically can not only boost their internal social programs but can also be leveraged to help nonprofit partners elevate their management.
- **Knowledge** and experience in consumer behavior, technology, distribution, communication, and first-hand customer contact enables insight into societal challenges at a local level, discover programs that will help, and find ways to adapt and scale those programs.
- **Agility**, which enables businesses to act quickly and to adapt programs to trends, events, and local conditions.
- **Offerings partially at fault.** Firm's role in creating or enabling problems such as obesity, teen self-image issues, energy waste and more are in a good position to make meaningful progress in addressing them.
- **A willingness to take risks** nursing promising methods and programs that may look like long shots. They also can choose to address societal problems that exist in poor populations that lack a political base. In contrast, government entities are generally more effective and more comfortable to scale proven solutions to societal problems that have visibility within a politically meaningful part of society.

The Gates Foundation. An influential role model and proof point for the professionalization of efforts to address social needs and issues was offered by the Bill and Melinda Gates Foundation, founded in 2000, but built on efforts in the prior decade.

Bill, the founder and long-time CEO of Microsoft, and Melinda were pressed by a friend to read an article in 1997 about the number of children dying around the world from diseases such as diarrhea and pneumonia, which were easily treated in wealthier countries. That led to a passion to help the poorest people live healthier and more productive lives through their foundation which was started with a 16-billion-dollar investment of Microsoft stock. During the early years, they expanded the scope to include the goal of strengthening the U.S. public education system, a driver of equality. A few years later, climate change and gender equality were added.

The Gates Foundation demonstrated how private firms and nonprofit entities could accomplish ambitious goals on their own or in partnership with government. Three observations were made about their methods and results that were influential in framing the way that social programs should be developed and run.

First, their approach uses basic good management principles that included staffing right, budgeting, and setting measurable progress goals. It starts with understanding the problem using both experts and on-the-ground research There was a lot of "listen and learn."

It included an exhaustive review of the existing approaches. What has been tried? What have been the roadblocks (taking a daily pill to avoid HIV was too much for the system to supply and for the recipient to take)? What are the barriers and how could they be overcome? What are available options?

If the existing approaches are not adequate, the foundation is ready to invest in modifying what exists or to invest in research to come up with a fresh approach. In fact, the foundation emphasizes its role to test out promising innovations, collect and analyze the data, and let businesses and governments scale up and sustain what works.

The Foundation, for example, ran an ongoing "Reinvent the Toilet Challenge" contest which started in 2011 to invent a new toilet that would remove harmful pathogens and recover energy, clean water, and nutrients, all without a connection to water and sewers, and with the requirement to run for under $0.05 a use. A decade later, there are more than 25 breakthrough prototypes available for commercialization by sanitation service companies, and several are in test markets.

Second, the Gates Foundation shows the power of collaboration. Nearly all their work is in collaboration with other partners including firms, communities, countries, and other nonprofits. In 2020, they had over 1,300 partners. A firm that is trying to impact a social problem does not have to go-it-alone. It can join the Gates Foundation family of partners.

Some of the alliances are major global efforts. The Gates Foundation was one of the founders and major funder of GAVI, the Vaccine Alliance, which jumpstarted an effort to vaccinate children in poor countries by bringing together key UN agencies, vaccine manufacturers, aid agencies, and major foundations to vaccinate children in poor countries. The Gates Foundation, in 2002, similarly was instrumental in creating the Global Fund to Fight AIDS, Tuberculosis, and Malaria, three diseases which were spiraling out of control in poor countries.

Other partners are with a single stand-alone nonprofit. The BAM (Becoming a Man) program helps young men in neighborhoods with a lot of crime and gang activity explore their emotions and hone their decision-making skills with group sessions twice a week for as much as a year. The Gates Foundation came to understand that advancing education in poor U.S. communities needed to deal with some of the contributing contexts such as the social/cultural route to crime, and BAM was in the mix. Those kids that participated in the BAM programs were half as likely to have trouble with the law.

Third, they showed that it is possible to take on huge programs with complexities and still succeed, often with quantitative evidence. Since 2000, Gavi has provided basic vaccines to more than 760 million children, prevented 13 million deaths, reduced the price of vaccine, in one case by 75%. Since 2002, Global Fund and its partners served over 150 countries with bed nets, AIDS treatments, TB tests, and other lifesaving solutions. It has disturbed over $45 billion, saving an astonishing 38 million lives and offering care, treatment, and prevention to hundreds of millions more. They clearly were willing to go for "home runs," to make the difficult doable.

Business Brands Need a Social Program Energy and Image Lift

Brands need energy to gain visibility and even the perception of success and being an innovative leader. Brands also need to improve or reinforce their image, usually an important part of the connection they have with employees, customers, and other stakeholders.

Creating energy and image lift is not easy in a world with information overload, media clutter, and pervasive perceived sameness. That is true for most brands but particularly true for brands that provide "taken for granted," functional benefits. These brands may be well-known and even liked but are out-of-mind, never talked about. As a result, customer ties are weak and vulnerable to a "fresh face" brand.

A signature social brand, a brand that is addressing a real need that attracts empathy with a unique program can provide a vehicle to create that elusive energy and image lift. Recall that Lifebuoy got 44 million views from three story videos that described the reactions of mothers living in villages that had received the "Help a Child Reach 5" program. This for a bar soap. The Dove Real Beauty and Self-Esteem numbers were even higher. In both cases, the brands got energy, inspiration, and a sense of shared values with key stakeholders from the signature social program.

Chapter 8 elaborates on how a signature social program can enhance a firm or business brand and why that is a motivation to pursue social program leadership.

Lessons from Historians

Historian Edward O'Donnell has observed that a significant change of historical note nearly always has multiple causes, is enabled by the will of groups of ordinary people as well as towering leaders, involves institutions and people that face difficult adaptation challenges, and is precipitated by a crisis situation. These four factors are present as we move from the shareholder to the stakeholder model with the presumption that firms now need to, and are capable of, taking on the serious challenges facing society, a significant change of historical note for sure.[58]

We now turn to Part II where, with context now on the table, attention turns to the three strategic thrusts that define the future of purpose-driven branding according to this book.

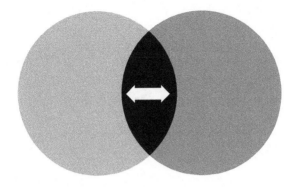

Part II
Signature Social Programs that Inspire, Impact, & Thrive

Most firms now aspire to have a robust, effective effort to address societal needs and issues, but few are close to reaching their potential. In Part II, the first of the three strategic thrusts needed to reach societal program leadership is presented—creating signature social programs that inspire, impact, and thrive.

Chapter 5 explains why a purpose or mission and culture is a necessary step to enable social programs to be developed and supported within an organization. Chapter 6 defines signature social programs, compares the experience of creating an internal program vs. adopting an external nonprofit partner, and discusses the challenge of managing the family of brands that will emerge. Chapter 7 addresses finding or creating signature social programs that can make a difference and represent the societal efforts of the firm or business. Parts III and IV will introduce the remaining two strategic thrusts, integrating the signature program into a business and developing a strong signature social brand.

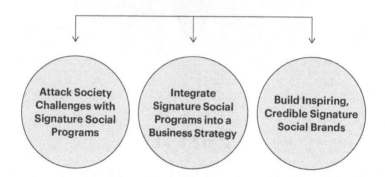

Chapter 5

PURPOSE/MISSION AND CULTURE THAT ENABLE AND INSPIRE SOCIAL PROGRAMS

Passion is energy, Feel the power from focusing on what excites you.

Oprah Winfrey

Prophet Impact—An Evolution

Prophet, the brand, growth, and transformation consulting firm with which I am associated, has long had a culture of being active with societal issues and programs. The signature social program at Prophet for over a decade was P4NP (Prophet for Nonprofits), where one day a year, consultant teams throughout the firm would focus on a problem holding back a nonprofit. A review suggested that this program would have more impact if it was not restricted to one day and if its focus was not only toward local charities. It was also clear that the societal charge needed to expand.

As a result, in 2021, the societal effort was expanded and branded as Prophet Impact. The P4NP day became Prophet Impact Day, a day that could be spent on community activities as well as on helping nonprofits. In addition, the VTO (volunteer time off) program was established whereby every employee could take an additional day off to volunteer to a nonprofit or help the community in some way. Then there is the Prophet Impact Auction, in which anything from brownies to vacation homes are auctioned off for a cause, such as supporting girls at a Tanzanian school.

But Prophet Impact had more. Prophet Pro Bono was launched where a consulting engagement would be set up for a nonprofit recruited by an interested Propheteer who may not have even had a contact at the nonprofit but believed in the mission. A toolkit was developed that showed how to select and approach such a nonprofit and what types of services might be offered. In addition, an environmental review of Prophet operations led to energy saving goals and initiatives.

In addition to Prophet Impact, a Chief Diversity Officer was added to lead the DEI effort (diversity, equity, and inclusion). Hiring goals, sensitivity initiatives, energizing the "women in leadership" effort, and town halls to discuss diversity and other societal issues of the day were instituted. Further, efforts to encourage and help clients be more aggressive and impactful in addressing society challenges were developed. All this made addressing societal needs become even more firmly a part of the firm's DNA.

This thrust was driven by a new firm purpose—to *"Unleash the power of people, businesses and brands to move society forward." It is uplifting, providing an answer to the "why" question. Why this company? Why should I come to work? Why should I admire what we do? "Unleash the power" represents energy. And importantly "moving society forward" provides an umbrella for the firm's societal effort and for making this effort a part of the strategy and culture.*

A firm's progress toward addressing and impacting the problems and issues facing society requires a shared belief within the firm that such an effort is supported and encouraged. It is not an appendage, but a part of the business strategy and culture.

This shared belief should not only be supported by role models such as Unilever and Salesforce, but also by the logic enunciated in the last chapter. The problems and issues such a climate change, inequality, and access to health and education affect are visible and . The firm will be responding to needs and demands of stakeholders, especially employees. And it can make a difference by leveraging its knowledge, resources, skills, and agility.

The belief should go beyond the rationale arguments. It should be supported by empathy and passion about individuals in need, a planet with growing environmental stresses, and a sometimes-desperate search for meaning in the professional life of people and organizations. Working to gain a paycheck and create wealth for shareholders is not inspiring or even satisfying whether you are an executive or on the front line. There needs to be a head and a heart behind the move to excel in the social realm.

There are many routes to get buy-in for the shared belief that programs that impact society should be part of the firm's DNA. Beliefs, values and goals are among the tools that can help but two stand out. The first is to create a purpose or mission that will inspire and guide that will become the head of the spear. The second, developing a culture that supports and even celebrates societal program initiatives, is the body of the spear.

Creating a Purpose or Mission that Nurtures Social Programs

Recall from Chapter 1 that a business's (or firm's) purpose or mission should be a high-level message about the essence of the business, which should inspire, feel authentic and be credible, guide decisions and initiatives, and be meaningfully worthwhile. In most contexts, the primary role of the purpose or mission is to inform, or more likely to remind, stakeholders about what the business, at its core, is all about. It should make prominent what it is about the business that distinguishes and inspires. In the case of Prophet, the "unleashing the power" and "move society forward" become part of how Prophet is framed in people's minds particularly the employees and partner organizations.

Recall also that the terms "purpose" and "mission" are here used interchangeably because some firms have committed to one of the two, because distinguishing between the two would be distracting, and because although they start from different perspectives, they both are capable of ending with an essence statement.

The purpose or mission usually takes the form of a punchy, clear, and memorable sentence but can also be longer or elaborated. It can take many different forms. It might emphasize, for example, the

- "Why?" question—why does the business exist?
- "What?" question—What does the business do or do well?
- "Goals" question—What is the future scenario?
- "Societal need question"—What is the commitment to addressing societal challenges? Which will be the focus?

Inspiration is a particularly important output of a purpose or mission, prompting sentiments such as: "This is a business that I admire, I am proud to be associated with, shares my values, and makes my work meaningful." "I understand why my company exists and why do I go to work." The purpose or mission is in a good position to inspire because it is at the front of the parade, and it does not have a broad communication brief. To inspire means getting beyond "what you do" to instill motivation for doing it. Not an easy task.

The "future of purpose-driven branding" argument, as outlined in Chapter 1, is that the purpose or mission as a high-status flag carrier should permit or encourage the organization to address societal problems and issues with programs that thrive. It needs to go beyond growth and profitability. Creating insanely great products is not enough.

Including a societal dimension into a purpose or mission can be accomplished in four ways:

- A business strategy is based on social purpose/mission
- A single purpose/mission that enables societal programs
- A social purpose/mission is one of multiple purpose/mission statements
- A corporate social purpose/mission sits beside a business purpose/mission.

A Business Strategy is Based on a Social Purpose/Mission

As noted in Chapter 1, when a business a strategy and brand position based on having an offering that is "green" or "healthy" or that addresses another societal concern, the purpose and mission will then include a social component as a major thrust of its business purpose or mission. Consider:

- Tesla: "*To accelerate the world's transition to sustainable energy,*"
- Patagonia: "*Save our home planet using our voice, our business and our community,*"
- Seventh Generation: "*We're on a mission to transform the world into a healthy, sustainable & equitable place for the next seven generations.*"

A Single Purpose or Mission Statement that Enables Social Programs

Many purpose or mission statements do enable social programs as well as serving as an inspirational guide to the business. That can sometimes be difficult and require an in depth understanding of the types of societal needs to address and the assets that can be brought to bear. Consider:

- Prophet: "*Unleash the power of people, businesses and brands to move society forward.*"
- Johnson & Johnson: "*We blend heart, science and ingenuity to change the trajectory of health for humanity.*"
- Starbucks: "*To inspire and help the human spirit—one person, one cup, and one neighborhood.*"
- Crayola: "*To help parents and teachers raise inspired, creative children.*"
- Goldman Sachs: "*to advance sustainable economic growth and financial opportunity across the globe.*"

They are all inspirational, guide strategic initiatives, and not only enable social programs but suggest what type of programs would fit and impact. With a supportive purpose or mission providing an internal rational to accept and grow new social programs, the argument shifts from "Why?" to whether this will work.

Multiple Purpose/Mission Statements

When the business purpose or mission cannot be stretched to cover societal needs, there is an alternative—to create a separate social purpose or mission. In that case, a business brand will have two or more hats, one or more that reflect its business and one or more that reflect its societal effort. When this happens, there is almost always a single brand that is being represented by more than one purpose or mission statements. There are many examples of firms that have done just that with different variations, some of which were introduced in chapter 1.

Ben and Jerry's, for example, has three statements, one representing the business, another the societal efforts and the third both.

- Product mission—*"We are driven to make fantastic ice-cream for its own sake."*
- Economic mission—*"We manage our company for sustainable economic growth."*
- Social mission—*"We are compelled to use our Company in innovative ways to make the world a better place."* The word compelling puts an umbrella around some disparate and quirky initiatives.

Caterpillar has four missions that inform strategies and decisions—to provide the best customer value, to grow, to develop and reward people, and to encourage social responsibility. The fourth mission reflects a dedication *"to improving the quality of life while sustaining the quality of our earth. We encourage social responsibility."*

Pepsico elaborates its mission for each of five stakeholder groups, thus creating five mission statements with the last two supporting social programs. The core mission. *"Create more smiles with every sip and every bite"* is whimsical and relies on the smile metaphor. Interpreting it for each stakeholder yields five mission statements:

- *"For our consumers—by creating joyful moments through our delicious and nourishing products and unique brand experiences."*
- *"For our customers (retailers)—by being the best possible partner, driving game-changing innovation, and delivering a level of growth unmatched in our industry".*
- *"For our shareholders—by delivering sustainable top-tier shareholder return and embracing best-in-class corporate governance"*
- *"For our employees and communities—by creating meaningful opportunities to work, gain new skills and build successful careers, and a diverse and inclusive workplace."*
- *"For our planet—by conserving nature's precious resources and fostering a more sustainable planet for our children and grandchildren."*

A Corporate Social Purpose/Mission Sits Beside a Business Purpose/ Mission

Another approach is to use the corporate brand to include the purpose or mission relevant to social programs. The business unit can then have flexibility to include or not include a societal dimensions.

Unilever. Recall that the mission of Unilever is "*We aim to make sustainable living commonplace with high-performing brands that are a force for good, taking action for a more sustainable and equitable world.*" *It features "sustainable living," "force for good," and a "more sustainable and equitable world." The 100 plus business units of Unilever thus can rely on the corporate mission to provide the organization backing to engage in aggressive societal programs. Their purpose or mission can, if convenient, focus on the business.*

Virgin Group brand. The Virgin brand begin in 1970 when Virgin Records was started now encompasses 40 major businesses that are all influenced by its purpose to "change business for good." They are also then given permission to develop their own purpose or mission. Virgin Atlantic Airlines, for example, has a mission to "grow a profitable airline where people love to fly and where people love to work."

The corporate purpose or mission can be housed in a corporate foundation as it was for Salesforce.

Salesforce, the foundation brand. As noted in Chapter 1, Salesforce has a business mission statement "*to empowers companies to connect with their customers in a whole new way.*" The Salesforce Foundation has a mission that is motivated by their belief that "Technology, when used for good, can change the world." Both serve to inspire, communicate how their resources and strategies can be employed, and guide innovative new programs. But there is one Salesforce brand and one culture that is informed by both mission statements and their supporting strategies and programs. Nether mission is of reduced priority and the foundation's staff and business organization work closely together.

Creating a purpose or mission that really clicks and fosters pride, empathy, energy, and direction while being clear and memorable is difficult and requires a deep understanding of the firm, its strategy, and its context with talent and patience to find the right thoughts and words. It can take time and productive workshops. There are few home run statements of purpose or mission and too many that are bland, understated, descriptive, uninspiring, or obsolete. The good news that it is worth trying and retrying because the right purpose and mission can really make a difference.

A purpose is powerful. Alan Jope, shortly after becoming Unilever COE in 2019, commented on the firm's "Sustainable Living Brands," brands that communicate a strong social purpose. He noted that—"We believe the evidence is clear and compelling that brands with purpose grow. Purpose creates relevance for a brand, it drives talkability, builds penetration, and reduces price elasticity."[59]

The Business and Social Purpose/Mission—Tradeoffs

There will be trade-offs between the business and the social purpose or mission that will occur whether they are operating under a separate purpose or mission or not. Neither can pretend to exist by itself. When there are conflicts and tradeoffs, they need to be handled by considering the long-term health of the business and the social programs. It might be that an action that appears suboptimal with respect to the business or a social program may in the long run be the sensible course. The social purpose or mission should get the right issues on the table at the right time but should not dictate or constrain.

Adapting the Culture

Organizational culture brings the purpose/mission and strategy to life. It is critical that the signature social programs find a role in the culture of the sponsoring organization. The culture is the beliefs, priorities, behaviors, and operating style that determine how the organization and its employees view, decide, feel, and act on issues and options that come before them. It reflects the "that is how we do things here" or "that is who we are."

A strong culture, one that is accepted and socially enforced, is important to an organizational success as many studies can attest. It makes employees more motivated and more likely to join and remain. It makes businesses more attractive to all its stakeholders. It clarifies communication about the business purpose or mission. If a program is supported by the culture, the wind will be at its back. Peter Drucker, the management guru of the last century, once said that "culture eats strategy for breakfast" which implies that having the right culture means that strategy will evolve and will be implemented with vigor.

Some elements of a culture are explicitly governed by a policy. If a person at Prophet needs to decide whether to take a day off to work on a nonprofit in trouble or to form a team to consult for a nonprofit, there is a policy for each, just go ahead. That has been decided. Much of a culture is not in any policy statement, however, some are not even articulated. Instead of a written policy and rules there is a shared instinct, well-known in the firm, as to what is the right decision, activities, or behavior. It just feels right, it feels like something others would back because of a long list of decisions, activities, and behaviors that have come before and provide a context.

Acceptance of a robust societal effort should be part of the culture as indicated by its purpose or mission, values, decisions, and behaviors. One study observed the culture at 230 firms and concluded that most cultures consist of one or more of eight styles—results focused (goals, execution), innovative (open, learning), enjoyment (playful, sense of humor), bold (decisive, risk taking), prepared (careful, safe), efficient (respectful, orderly), caring (teamwork, trust, belonging), and purpose (sustainability & social responsibility).[60] It is important that caring and purpose be a strong part of the culture.

How can an organization create or support a culture friendly to societal efforts? Three suggestions.

First, **CEO support.** The top executives and especially the CEO has to signal that societal efforts are part of the DNA, the soul, the purpose or mission, of the business. The signature social programs should carry the flag, that is one of their jobs. They represent authenticity, credibly, uniqueness and impact. The CEO and team should regularly talk about them, include them as part of the firm's strategy, and have their enhancements and successes recognized. It should be clear that these programs are prioritized and resourced.

Second, **buy-in**. There needs to be buy-in by employees and other stakeholders as to how meaningful the societal needs are and how impactful the programs will be. If the program is unknown or "foreign," there will be an absence of support and maybe even suspicion that the effort is secondary. In particular:

- Communicate the signature programs through all the employee communication channels including the website, townhalls, podcasts, and planning meetings. What is unique and impressive about them? What is new? What are the successes? Give a voice to the champions of the signature programs. Assign an executive to promote a pillar of a signature program brand.

- Find and use memorable signature stories. Prophet has a Prophet Impact Day story bank. One involved helping an organization tasked with promoting STEM learning. A brand strategy was advanced together with wording that communicated and a social media strategy. The story gets through, provides clarity, and is remembered. Chapter 12 elaborates.

- Create or elevate an executive position in the organization, such as a Chief Social Impact Officer, that would signal that social programs are part of the DNA of the organization

Third, **engagement and passion**. Culture needs to live all through the organization but there also needs to be a core base of employees that have gone beyond buy-in to having passion and being engaged. The task is to encourage active participation in the programs. Identify leaders and champions of the programs who will drive programs to not only succeed but to the be accepted and valued. The total social effort should be known, but it is the signature programs that should be the focus. Some basics:

- Create engagement through focused volunteering efforts involving teams of employees and perhaps customers.

- Create communities around the societal needs that are the focus. Prophet, for example, has teams and town halls that focus on women in management and diversity realities and challenges.

- For external signature programs, create visibility and involvement with an annual nonprofit fundraising event.

Creating and nurturing a culture are brand building tasks. Thus, many of the concepts and tools covered in the six chapters of Part III of the book can be applied.

The next chapter will turn to the centerpiece construct of the book, the signature social program and brand.

Chapter 6

THE SIGNATURE SOCIAL PROGRAM

A brand that captures your mind gains behavior, a brand that captures your heart gains commitment.

Scott Talgo, Brand Strategist

Goldman Sachs--Social Programs that Inspire, Impact and Fit

1 0,000 Women. In 2008, Goldman Sachs (Goldman) launched 10,000 Women with a long-term commitment to support women entrepreneurs throughout developing countries. The number 10,000 highlighted their goal of reaching 10,000 women entrepreneurs. Motivated by the ongoing voice of professional women at Goldman and elsewhere and supported by a firm's "inclusive growth" social purpose, it was influenced by a Goldman study with the World Bank. This study revealed that women leading small and medium sized firms in developing countries had a 1.5 trillion-dollar deficit in accessing debt and correcting that would lead to a 12% increase in personal income in these countries and many more jobs where they are needed.

The core idea was to establish a certificate business management programs with courses such as marketing, accounting, market research, writing a business plan, strategic planning, accessing capital, and e-commerce. These programs, with guidance and participation of professors from top business schools plus Goldman mentors, provided opportunities for women to gain practical business skills but, more important, confidence and credibility. Local colleges throughout the world delivered the courses. When the pandemic hit, the courses went online, and the number served was expanded.

In 2014, Goldman developed a finance facility labeled WEOF (Women Entrepreneurs Opportunity Facility) with the International Finance Corporation (IFC), a member of the World Bank Group, to provide financing and expertise through local banks to these same women entrepreneurs in emerging markets. A goal was to provide financing but also to demonstrate the commercial viability of investing in women. In the first five years, more than 50,000 loans averaging $25,000 were made to women.

Students and graduates got access to an alumni network community with all the benefits of giving and getting helpful information and advice. They could exchange ideas about how to export, build a brand, or expand an e-commerce business. And they could do business with each other, in fact over 80% did just that. The community also provided invaluable social support. They were not in this alone. The 10,000 Women Growth Fellowships was added to provide selected women alumni with an intensive program of events held over three days with coaching sessions, collaborative training, Goldman mentoring, and networking.

The 10,000 women programs did reach its goal of affecting 10,000 entrepreneurial businesses by 2021, a goal which was then doubled. And there was leverage. The average graduate became a mentor to nine people, so the effect was far beyond the 10,000 businesses. The program platform provided a foundation to two additional programs.

10,000 Small Business Program. In 2009, there was a financial meltdown and U.S. small business owners were particularly hard hit. In response, Goldman introduced the 10,000 Small Business Program with a set of courses on running and growing a business offered through junior colleges, an ongoing webinar series, mentoring from Goldman employees, access to capital through the

CDFI (Community Development Financial Institutions), and a Small Business Resource Center that had frequently updated suggestions on how a small business could grow its sales, address problems, and access government programs. The program was expanded to include 10,000 Small Businesses Voices that provide tools and training to help program alumni advocate for policy changes affecting their businesses and communities and the #MakeSmallBig virtual marketplace to enable the Small Business alumni community access to markets.

The program got traction. In 2020, 11 years after founding, it had made loans to 17,000 businesses (well beyond the goal) averaging over $50,000 per loan. Its influence was also leveraged as over 50% of the participants were, or became, a community leader and 75% mentored another.

One Million Black Women. Goldman's research revealed that black women's hourly earnings gap is 15% lower than white women and 35% lower when compared with white men. Further, only 0.5% of single Black women own their own business, a rate 24 times lower than for single white men. As a result in 2021, Goldman launched the One Million Black Women program in the U.S. with a commitment to provide $10 billion in financial support plus $100 million in supporting programs over the ensuing ten years to reduce the barriers that lie behind the racial wealth disparity. The program targeted financial health, digital connectivity, housing, jobs, healthcare, education, as well as access to capital for Black women. Success will mean not only a better life for these women and the people and organizations they touch but also an estimated $350 to $450 billion added to the US GNP and as many as 1.7 million new U.S. jobs.

These three signature social programs were supported by Goldman's expertise and power in the capital markets and fit their mission to promote inclusive growth to provide ways for those left behind to surge (a second social mission focused on climate change). Each addresses a major societal problem that had a visibility surge and did with audacious goals and scope. Note how the strategy of the first was adapted to the other two; how partners, particularly colleges and financial entities, enabled the programs; and how the programs evolved over time. These programs dramatically carry the flag for the inclusive thrust of Goldman and importantly demonstrate how the Goldman culture and style can be leveraged to address societal problems.

Signature Social Programs

Signature social programs have two jobs that require their signature status. Job 1 is to make a meaningful, convincing impact on a challenging problem facing society at large by providing guidance and inspiration. The signature status will mean that the program is meaningful and visible, that it is focused and well-resourced, that it is supported by a long-term commitment, and there is real impact.

Job 2 is to enhance a partner firm or business by creating energy, an image lift, and a strong connection with employees and other stakeholders. Job 2 is the lynchpin of any effort to integrate the signature program with a business strategy creating a team effort.

In the absence of a signature program, the societal effort of a firm or business would usually involve a description of volunteering hours, grant money spent, and possibly energy use goals resulting in what appears to be a fragmented, ad hoc effort that does not sound different than other firms. There would be little understanding as to what societal problems were addressed, what impact was made, or that the effort represented a significant commitment for the firm given its size. As a too-common result, there is no energy, no sense of urgency, no feeling of making a difference, no emotional connection, and no feeling of pride. Only a diffuse and forgettable set of facts.

A signature social program and its associated social brand will have an unique ability to breakthrough information overload, media clutter, and perceived "sameness and puffery." It can represent and add credibility to the total societal effort of a firm or business by its ability to provide "proof points" about the commitment of the firm or business to make a difference.

What exactly is a signature social program. To be precise, as Figure 6-1 shows, a signature social program

- Will address a **societal challenge that touches people**. It is real and feels real emotionally. It aims to make the world better rather than just striving to operate up to legal or ethical standards. It comes to life. For the "Help a Child Reach 5" program it might be based on a specific set of stories about how individuals were affected by the difficulty of obtaining clean water. Or by that fact that 2 million kids under 5 die each year. Or in the case of a program such as Pledge 1%, it is a vivid understanding of the enormity of societal challenges such as of global warming and inequality and the importance of taking action over a broad front.

- Is **credible, impactful, and committed**. Credibility comes in part from what the programs does. Does it have face validity? Does the concept seem logical and workable? Has it got a creative twist that makes its contribution unique and intriguing? Has it demonstrated competence and impact? Is it resourced? Is there a committed partner organization? Has it been in operation for an extended period? Does it show commitment by its investment? Does it have or aspire to have a leadership position.

- Will **lift the energy and image of a business**. The interest and respect that it engenders will benefit a sponsoring business brand. The signature social program can demonstrate that the business is not just about growing sales and profits accepts an obligation to address societal challenges and thus instill respect and even inspiration. A signature program can also add energy and visibility to a business. Just consider the Lifebuoy boost that came from three "Help a Child Reach 5" videos that received 44 million views. Chapter 8 elaborates.

- Has a **visible, inspiring brand** that will guide the program, motivate the staff, and lead its dual communication task. First, to staff, the clients, and other people and organizations that make the program successful. Second, to the sponsoring business and their employees and stakeholders. In both cases, a brand can aid communication by providing credibility and context for the processing of new information. The brand needs to find and leverage elements of the societal need or of the program itself that stands out, that will attract interest, and start a conversation. There has to be a reason to know about the brand and to have a connection to it. Part III of the book provides a roadmap to building a signature social program brand.

- Can be **internal** (such as Lifebuoy's H is for Handwashing program) or an **external nonprofit** (Doctors Without Borders) programs reflecting an engaged long-term partner commitment by a business.

Figure 6-1

SIGNATURE SOCIAL PROGRAM

Internal vs. External Signature Social Programs

We can distinguish between two types of signature social programs that are often the major options when finding and selecting a credible program that impacts, inspires, and aids a business. Each has its own strengths and challenges.

The internal option

One alternative is to create, resource, and manage a signature social program and brand. As we saw with Lifebuoy's "Help a Child Reach 5", the Dove Self-Esteem program, Salesforce's Nonprofit Cloud, and the Goldman programs, there are benefits from having a "wholly owned" internal program. There is an ability to evolve the program, making it more and more impactful. With control over its resources and operations, the risk of failing to exploit growth options or faltering is reduced. And the pride and heritage of creation can inspire employees and stakeholders. Finally, there is the clear ownership that can help its ability to help a sponsoring business.

It is not easy. There are numerous societal needs and issues, but finding one or more that is substantial enough and fits your firm or business can be elusive. A program that reaches a small target and is not scalable or connects with a small part of the business will be of limited value. Further, there are questions to address. Have others preempted the idea? Can our firm execute it? Are the resources available? Can the program brand be established? Will the result be worth the effort and cost? Can a fit with the business be created? Is the cost commitment over time feasible? These uncertainties can make an internal program that really impacts and connects to stakeholders difficult to identify and implement and sometimes simply not feasible.

To add to the difficulty—a program is rarely born already fully grown and mature. It will take time for it to reach its potential with a lot of learning and adapting along the way. That means that a considerable amount of projecting is needed in understanding how a program, some in the embryonic idea stage, might evolve and, in the process, overcome some perceived limitations or liabilities. A commitment decision can be risky.

The external option

The alternative is to find an existing external social program with an established brand and purpose or mission that has been tested and fits within the business. The external program, usually a nonprofit, then becomes a signature program for the sponsoring firm. A proven program with a strong brand and clear associations means that most of the task has been accomplished and the risk of a disappointing outcome is reduced. The challenge is then to link the brand to the business by carving out a unique sponsorship role and making the association visible and memorable, usually a much more manageable task than creating a new program and brand.

Home Depot, for example, has partnered with Habitat for Humanity, a proven, admired brand with a demonstrably effective and efficient program.

Home Depot has developed its own niche within the partnership, "Homes for Veterans." Habitat is a proven, admired brand. The task for Home Depot is to become an active partner with a long-term perspective that will provide organizational resources (like employee volunteers and building expertise and materials) and a common passion about building homes. The key is to become an active partner and not a passive giver of a grant.

Umbrella Brands

We have been talking about finding, creating, or partnering with a branded signature social program that could be external or internal. Each could make a powerful statement. But there is also a need for umbrella brands, that sometimes could be termed umbrella programs, that cover more than a single signature social program. These brands could have signature status if they provide a source pride and credibility to a sponsoring firm or business. Consider two types—those that allow unbranded programs to find a voice and those that provide a logical theme for a broader effort involving branded and unbranded programs.

A Voice for Unbranded Social Efforts

Much of the societal effort will be unbranded or branded with a weak descriptive brand. Often the volunteering of employees, dispersed grants to nonprofits, changes to operations to reduce carbon emission or energy use, employee policies, and much more, for example, will not operate under a strong brand. So how to get credit for that?

One path is to create an umbrella brand that will span unbranded social efforts. The scope can vary. Salesforce has its Citizen Philanthropists as an umbrella brand covering the volunteer efforts of its employees and Goldman Sachs has had the Community TeamWorks since 1997 that has the same function. The challenge is to communicate a societal need and social program for a group of actions that may be wildly dispersed. Stories from a few of them, even though different, can support the umbrella brand communicating the type of activity that being pursued and its impact.

Umbrella Brands to Represent Multiple Signature Programs

An even more important problem is often created by the existence of many signature programs along with unbranded efforts. In that case there are multiple brands to deal with that raises several issues and challenges that an umbrella social brand can address, a brand that can assume signature status in some contexts.

Salesforce, for example, has a need to communicate to its employees and other stakeholders its commitment to address societal problems. It has many signature social programs which by themselves represent an incomplete and confused message. There is less synergy and build as a result. The solution is to have Salesforce, in addition to being business brand, take on the role of a umbrella social brand.

The firm or business brand thus assumes two roles, that of a business brand and a social effort brand, a not uncommon occurrence. Recall in Chapter 5 the concept of a firm having a social purpose side-by-side with a business purpose. The firm or business brand then captures all the social effort of the firm and as multiple signature programs and unbranded efforts get communicated and connected the total impact grows and not just in an additive way. Together, a team of many signature programs can create a strong overall message that would otherwise not be possible with one or two players.

Goldman, for example, has the three signature programs described at the outset of this chapter. Ben & Jerry's (from Chapter 2) have a bewildering array of social efforts but all with an underlying force and style. Patagonia, as we shall see in Chapter 11, has eye-opening signature programs that span issues and methods. The Salesforce brand is defined by Pledge 1%, Philanthropy cloud, the Nonprofit Cloud, the Education Cloud, and many others. In each case, these firm brands provide an umbrella signature brand to represent what is common to all those signature social programs as well as other efforts not branded.

For the corporate brand itself to be a umbrella social brand means that role needs to be actively managed. Its link to the signature social programs and other efforts must be established. People have to know that it is a Patagonia social program or a Ben & Jerry's initiative. And the effort needs to become a driver of the purpose and culture of the organization.

The corporate brand could play that role but an umbrella brand dedicated to presenting the societal efforts of the firm can also play that role with less ambiguity. The Unilever Compass (or USLP), for example, covers all the social activities of the firm that has hundreds, maybe many hundreds of signature programs. Any exposure to one of these programs then enhances the umbrella brand.

Communicating the societal effort of the Unilever Compass is aided, as noted in Chapter 1, by breaking down the effort into three priority areas—Health, Confidence & Wellness; the Health of the Planet; and a Fairer, More Socially Inclusive World. Each area has subareas which can each act as an umbrellas brand. The first area, for example, includes Positive Nutrition (less salt, fat, sugar, etc.), Hygiene (handwashing), Clean Water, Sanitation, and Self-esteem. The labels are an important part of the communication effort for the Compass brand, helping to communicate what is being done and its impact. The umbrella brand, Compass, can demonstrate that the whole is more than the sum of its parts and that one or two impressive programs are not outliers but are representative of who Unilever is. It is the whole that reflects on Unilever.

Prophet Impact, from the last chapter, was another such umbrella brand. The social impact of Prophet could be communicated by the signature social programs that are Prophet Impact subbrands such as Prophet Impact Day, Prophet Impact Pro Bono, and Prophet Impact Auction. The resulting brand team provides an overall thrust and sense of commitment and it provides both vertical and horizontal support for each of the subbrand signature programs. NBA Cares (shown in the insert) is another example. The foundation can sometimes play that role as well, simultaneously representing a corporation and its societal efforts.

A smaller grouping of signature social programs could have a more focused goal. In Chapter 8 the combination of four programs by Barclays into one, the Digital Eagles, formed to help people thrive in a digital world, is an example.

NBA CARES—IDENTIFYING A SIGNATURE SOCIAL PROGRAM

NBA (National Basketball Association) Cares, launched in 2005, is the league's global program addressing social needs and issues driving the league's mission to "inspire and connect people everywhere through the power of basketball." One NBA Cares objective is to provide functional support, direction, and alignment to the NBA family which includes the league, teams, players, legends, coaches, referees, staff, community, and business partners who want to help those in need. A second is to serve as an umbrella brand to communicate and "story tell" the many efforts to address societal needs and issues by all members of this family.

NBA Cares has well over a dozen branded programs such as NBA Green, Hoops for Troops, NBA Fit, NBA Cares Season of Giving, NBA Cares Community Assist Programs, Building Bridges through Basketball, Mind Health, NBA Math Hoops and more. To support these initiatives, NBA Cares has engaged a host of partners that include Boys & Girls Clubs of America, Vera Institute of Justice, Thurgood Marshall College Fund, UNICEF, Special Olympics, and Share Our Strength.

It is not possible to communicate all these programs plus those of the members of the NBA family. NBA Cares steps in to play an important umbrella brand role. But there is still a need to assign signature status to a few of the programs to make sure that there is impact and that it is communicated. What should be the signature social brands that best illustrate what NBA Cares and the NBA in general is all about? Two candidates stand out—Live, Learn or Play Centers and the All-Star Day of Service—because of their visibility, impact, emotional connection, and communicability.

NBA Cares Live, Learn or Play Centers, created by the NBA family, such as libraires, technology labs, teen centers, mindfulness wellness rooms, renovated homes, and basketball courts represent an effort to create lasting community legacies. The first was installed in 2005 in New York City and 17 years later, at the All-Star game in Cleveland, the 2,000th center was dedicated. The Live, Learn or Play Center program deserves signature status because of its ongoing visible impact, the fact that it says global in a compelling way with projects in 40 countries and territories, and because its stories about centers particularly in marginalized neighborhoods in underdeveloped countries are powerful.

The NBA Cares All-Star Day of Service started in 2007 at the All-Star game in New Orleans as a way for the NBA family to assist the city's relief efforts following Hurricane Katrina. Every year since, there is a comparable volunteer effort by the NBA family during the NBA All-Star weekend with hands-on service specific to the All-Star game host community. The annual event shows the players, the legends, and the whole NBA family interacting with the community, providing their time and effort to improve the life, living space, and facilities of those in need. The program provides stories with a personal touch illustrating that the NBA is bigger than basketball.

A signature social program needs to be defined for the target audience. NBA Fit and NBA Math Hoops, for example, could have signature status for the audience for which they were created. For a focused target audience, the cost of building and maintaining a signature brand may be small, but having that role in that context is still helpful in managing the brand portfolio.

Managing the Team of Signature Social Programs

Creating and leveraging a single signature program is at the core of a social leadership strategy. But these programs are rarely alone, in most cases there are several signature programs and sometimes many often involving a mix of internal and external programs. This group of signature social programs becomes a team that needs to be actively managed so that each understands its role, its importance, and the relationship they have with each other and other elements of the sponsoring business that become team members as well.

Signature Programs Relationship with Each Other and the Firm

Companion or sister signature social programs should work together to achieve synergy and clarity thereby reducing costs, increasing their impact, and expanding their reach. They should avoid getting in each other's way by creating competition and confusion. For this to happen, the opportunities and risks associated with multiple signature social programs need to be actively managed. For example, consider the ability of one program to help another by:

Providing motivation. The Dove Real Beauty program with its eye-opening insights provides motivation and support for the Dove Self-Esteem program. Without the Real Beauty platform, there would not be the emotional tailwind or rationale that made the Self Esteem program so successful. And the existence of the Dove Self-Esteem program means that the impact from the Real Beauty program is much enhanced. There is a second chapter. As the result, keeping both alive and coordinated is a task that will continue to pay dividends.

Expanding the scope. The "Help a Child Reach 5" signature social program for Lifebuoy received substance and support from "The Global Handwashing Day." The touch of the "Help a Child Reach 5" program expanded globally and received visibility and stature from the association. The NBA Cares family all provides a unique set of social needs and audiences. Each one by itself is limited but as a group they have much more impact.

Providing credibility. Some signature social programs can provide credibility to others. The Pledge 1% (or 1-1-1) gets credibility from virtually all the signature social programs of Salesforce many of which can be quantified to demonstrate that the Pledge 1% has been exceeded.

Providing vertical clarity. Some signature social programs have others under them. For Salesforce the Power of Us provides not only free or reduced priced software, it also links four societal oriented software packages—Nonprofit

Cloud, Education Cloud, Philanthropy Cloud and Sustainability Cloud. It provides one way to create horizontal credibility. The four cloud programs help provide credibility to each other and substance to the Power of Us program. Prophet Impact also has signature programs under its wing that have subbrands such as Prophet Impact Day and Prophet Impact Auction.

Adapting a Program's Approach for New Arenas. Goldman developed the 10,000 women in 2008 that involved the use of business management instruction, mentoring, and financing help to women in underdeveloped countries. Those basic pieces were adapted to the 2009 10,000 Small Business Program and in 2021 to the One Million Black Women programs. This enabled the new societal arenas and provided on-going synergies.

Silver bullet brands. A signature social program can have branded feature, service, founder, story, or endorsers that provide energy, differentiation, or credibility. The brand and siliver bullet status insures that they are not neglected or under-resourced. They could be a "secret sauce" that addressed the questions, "Why this program?" More in Chapter 14.

Sharing resources. Any time resources needed for operations or brand building can be shared among signature social programs the result can be cost savings and a step-up in quality of execution. The Salesforce cloud brands under the Power of One could share graphics, a website, and even content because the explanation of what they do will have commonalities. The three Goldman programs could share training content and processes, staff, and client relationship techniques.

There is also the relationship of signature social programs with other branded programs in the firm or business. Salesforce utilizes the Trailblazer training modules and brand community as one pillar of their business strategy. Trailblazer is also employed as part of the firm's societal effort by making it available to those that need a lift to join the software workforce, some in underdeveloped countries. Thus, Trailblazer becomes a signature social program for Salesforce that is integrated into the Salesforce strategy and culture.

Making Resource Allocation Decisions

When there are several or many signature social programs there will be an implicit or explicit resource allocation to be made. How should resources be allocated between them? The basic analysis will consider the importance of the programs vs. its cost in resources.

All signature social programs are not equal. Some are simply more important than others because of their impact on societal needs (Job 1) or on enhancing a business (Job 2). There are levels of "signatureness." Exactly what is the potential for a program to do good for society and to help a business brand?

The evaluation then looks to the cost and resources needed to implement the program and build its brand. That in turn is affected by how the program is implemented and the needs of its brand building effort. Some programs can be adapted with modest budget needs. Others have substantial and require ongoing needs for resources.

At the end of the day, there may be a resource allocation decision to make between signature social programs. In the NBA Cares case, shown in the insert, two of their social programs were give signature status and the highest priority because of their visibility, impact, emotional connection, and communicability. These programs were well publicized and fully supported. There were other programs that involved a reduced footprint. Because their budget and resource needs were modest and they could still be eligible to have signature status albeit at a lessor level and for a smaller target audience.

At Salesforce, the Pledge 1% would be an important signature social program for a broad audience because its brand has a high level of energy and ability to represent the Salesforce commitment to do social good. The Education Cloud, the Nonprofit Cloud, and the Philanthropic Cloud would have signature status albeit at a reduced priority and scope because the resources they need are relatively modest and shared by other social and business programs.

Making a Signature Social Program Effective

A signature social program requires knowledge, insight, competence, strategic guidance and much more to be effective, to do its job. Three fundamental challenges stand out.

- **Finding the right programs.** Chapter 7 discusses how to find the right program, one that will impact, inspire, and fit the business. It is not easy finding an internal program that is "not taken and "doable" or an external program which can create a meaningful niche for your firm.
- **Integrating into a business.** Chapter 8 shows how a signature social program can advance the energy, image, and employee and customer connections to a business brand. Chapter 9 explains how the business brand can contribute an endorsement in addition to resources to a the signature social program. It is a win-win edge that should not be missed.
- **Building a strong brand.** Part III describes how a signature social program can build a strong brand that is the key ingredient to its success. Impacting a societal need and enhancing a business requires that the signature program be positioned and communicated, both branding tasks.

Chapter 7

FIND SIGNATURE SOCIAL PROGRAMS THAT INSPIRE, IMPACT AND FIT

The question is not what you look at but what you see.
Henry David Thoreau

Walmart's Transformation

Walmart's environmental awakening started in 2004 when the chairman, Rob Walton, took camping trips with the CEO of Conservation International. During their fireside chats, Walton was challenged to do something to preserve the trails, the woods, the air, and the natural environment in general. Intrigued, Walton embarked on a year of research and study after which he and Walmart made a commitment to accept the challenge.

What followed was a major corporate sustainability initiative involving employees, trucks, stores, warehouses, suppliers, communities, and customers. Fourteen teams—consisting of Walmart employees plus suppliers, environmental groups, and regulators—were formed to focus on sustainability in areas such as store operations, logistics, and the products in the store which involved their sourcing, packaging, the use of forest products, pesticides, and more.

The results were an amazing array of environmental programs with dramatic impact. What was surprising was the positive impact on business performance. Unexpectedly, there was a high level of cost savings, higher sales led by customer reaction to the environmentally friendly product mix, a reduction in the negative press about issues such as employee and suppler policies that had hounded the firm, and a brand image that was dramatically improved. One article that emerged was entitled "Green Project Making It Harder to Hate Walmart."[6162]

Since 2005, the Walmart environmental effort has grown in scope, impact, and aspirations. Project GigatonTM launched in 2017, for example, aims to avoid one billion metric tons (a gigaton) of greenhouse gases entering the global value chain by 2030. The program engages suppliers, challenging them to set goals to improve the environmental impact of their operations in key areas such as energy use, waste, and packaging. Over 3,000 suppliers came on board, and over 500 were named Giga Gurus because they established goals and were measuring progress. Walmart itself set dozens of goals. In 2022, for example, the firm had a goal of zero emissions from operations by 2040 and by 2030, they would protect, manage, or restore 40 million acres of land and 1 million square miles of ocean.

Walmart's transformation has been astounding. It does appear that they could have had an easier time inspiring and communicating if they had branded more of their efforts. The Project GigatonTM, that appeared well over a decade after the awakening, was a brand that made a difference in explaining the level of their aspiration and commitment. They did have external programs such as the Global Forest Watch that provides data and insights to protect forestation. But the major flagbearer of the Walmart environmental effort was the Walmart brand itself acting as an societal umbrella brand.

A business needs to create, elevate, or find signature social programs or groups of programs that will stand out on three dimensions. First, it should address a societal need or issue that is emotionally relatable, intriguing, and involving. Second, the program, whether internal or with an external nonprofit, should be credible, distinctive, and impactful. It should aspire to Wow!. Third, it should lend itself to being integrated into the strategy and culture of a business.

How to find such a program? The good news is there are many sources of options. We start with the major societal challenges and then discuss founder/CEO insights, employee initiatives, customer interests, suppliers, new technology/innovations, existing programs that may be hidden or underleveraged, and a firm's heritage, assets/expertise, and offerings.

Analyze the Major Societal Challenges

Reviewing the major needs, problems, and issues facing society such as climate change, inequality, health, and education, all described in Chapter 4, can generate options with attractive properties. First, the existence and importance of the societal need or problem is already widely recognized, it does not have to be explained. Second, there will be adherents who will be candidates for a brand community with a willingness to volunteer or donate. Third, there will be a host of nonprofits attracted to the need that can become external signature social programs or become an internal program's partner.

Climate change. Environmental programs have the advantage of addressing the most visible vexing long-term societal challenge: global warming. There are several ways in which firms make a difference with environmental programs.

First, they can look to their offerings or operations for ways to reduce energy use, CO_2 emissions, non-biodegradable plastics, dangerous pollutants, and water consumption. These are rarely branded or distinctive, although some umbrella goals can act as a brand. Microsoft, for example, was rated as the top stock with respect to ESG measures and financials by Investors Daily in 2021, a rating in large part due to an ambitious goal of getting itself and its supply chain carbon negative by 2030.[63]

A second way is to create offerings that are "green" and therefore advance environmental goals. They could include cleaning products that are free from contaminating ingredients or electric cars that emit low or no cardon emissions. Being "green" can provide self-expressive benefits. Buying and using Method Bathroom Cleaner or driving a Tesla can demonstrate to you and others a willingness to do something about the environment. Tesla has made sustainability the firm's core mission with its battery powered car and its initiatives to manufacture batteries and solar cells panels. GE has similarly created a substantial business by providing clean energy products such as windmills.

The third are programs that encourage the public or other firms to support open spaces, plant trees, use less energy, avoid materials that pollute, etc. In each case, the effort can be branded and made visible externally, thus enhancing the brand of the sponsoring firm or business. Patagonia's Worn Wear, where used clothing is reused or recycled, is one example and the creation of two protected parks by Muji, the Japanese retailer, is another.

With environmental programs, there is the risk that what seems helpful to the environment may have second or third order effects that will reduce or nullify the benefit. A new package may be better environmentally until you factor in the energy cost of making it. It turns out that planting the wrong trees in the wrong place can disturb the environmental balance and result in less forest density. So, it is complicated, and first impressions are not always enough.

Health. AbbVie has a mission to address the health needs of the underserved with multiple programs, a mission that fits and leverages the firm's expertise. A significant effort to address neglected tropical diseases is coordinated by the AbbVie Executive Council for Neglected Tropical Diseases (NTD). One aspect is a volunteer effort by AbbVie researchers outside working hours to create NTD medicines that will be effective. Another program goes beyond NTDs and supervises the donation of medicines in over 100 countries. There is the Good to Grow program in 20 countries that supports collaboration to address causes of preventable neonatal mortality for premature infants. Several AbbVie programs have, for decades, supported efforts to deal with HIV infections. AbbVie also has employee health programs like AbbVie Vitality (health seminars and promotions) and AbbVie in Motion (a four-week fitness regimen).

Education. HP has a long-standing reputation as being "good guys," as represented by the "HP Way," which has endured. One signature program is HP Life, a free online set of 25 courses available in 7 languages, geared to entrepreneurs or potential entrepreneurs. It was developed in conjunction with EDC, a nonprofit that designs and implements such programs. The opportunity to usher in a new era in global entrepreneurship by leveraging e-learning was the inspiration. During the first nine years since it began in 2012, 1.3 million people have participated from over 200 countries and many have joined a global community of entrepreneurs.

The list could on and on. The challenge is to find and occupy a niche within a societal need that has not gotten widespread attention, a niche in which your firm can both contribute and own. Even if only a small number are affected, an effective program can make a difference and create intriguing stories.

The Founder or CEO Insight

It is remarkable how the birth of many programs follows a pattern. A top executive, likely the founder or CEO, experiences a triggering event whereby a social problem or issue is seen up close and made personal. There is a "someone needs to do something" moment. That happened at Walmart. Other examples:

- Doniece Sandoval, who after hearing a homeless person mention a fear of never being clean again, decided to start Lava Mae (describe in more detail in Chapter 14), which provided showers to the homeless.
- Toms' founder saw children without shoes in an underdeveloped country and resolved to act—the result was a shoe company which, for every shoe sold, gave a pair away to those without. Dozens of firms making products from eyeglasses to socks have copied the idea.
- Marc Benioff, stimulated by an idea from a Guru in India about doing social good and developing a successful business, developed the 1-1-1 (now the Pledge 1%) model as described in Chapter 3.
- Bill Gates and his wife were told about the deaths throughout the world that were preventable if existing treatments could be scaled and jumpstarted. The result was an ambitious effort to do just that.
- When Cisco thought that distributing computers to schools would cut into the access deficiency but then found that they needed more than hardware, they created a program to provide user know-how.

In each case, it was an incident that made a social need visible and suggested the idea that a feasible solution was possible in the hands of a person capable of finding the organizational resources and commitment to make it happen.

Look to Employees, Customers, Suppliers, Technology & Existing Programs

Employee Initiatives. There are two ways to create a program as was noted in Chapter 2. The first, such as Dove's Self Esteem program, is top down where the organization determines a social or environmental problem and develops programs to deal with it.

The second is bottom up where the organization is a central broker finding organizational resources for solid ideas that emanate from employees or customers. Most firms have a significant part of their societal effort under the control of individual employees who look to a societal need or issue for which they have passion. As noted in Chapter 3, at Salesforce, employees have 1% (actually more than 1%) of their time to locate and deliver a program such as helping schools with disadvantaged kids or volunteering for a nonprofit that provides food for the needy. In each case, an individual employee decides if the effort is worthwhile, if it fits, and if he or she can deliver. Employees can also have any donations matched by Salesforce up to $5,000 (or more if supported by a proposal). This Salesforce employee effort has an umbrella brand Salesforce Citizen Philanthropists.

A small and embryonic employee effort around an existing nonprofit can lead to a firm's external partnership. Salesforce has a partnership with CoderDojo, who hosts free, volunteer-led, community-based programming clubs for young people, called Dojos, where 7–17-year-olds learn how to code, develop websites, apps, programs, games and explore technology in an informal and creative environment. Salesforce employees run Dojos, each led by a Salesforce "champion" and manned by Salesforce Dojo certified volunteers.

Customer Interests. Another approach is to look to your customers. What societal problems or issues would they connect with and value? Home Depot customers are do-it-yourselfers, so they can relate to active support of Habitat for Humanity. Avon's Breast Cancer Crusade, with its iconic Avon Walk for Breast Cancer that ran for over 12 years, had little link with the product or the capabilities of Avon, but it did connect with a concern close to most women, many of which have seen breast cancer up close through the experience of a friend or family member.

California Casualty Insurance Company serves groups such as teachers and patrolman. One program was providing teddy bears for the patrolman to give to kids that were experiencing trauma from an accident or other incident. That provided a softening of the impact and a sense of warmth to all involved. Another provided a redo of a school's teacher lounge, which is a source of social support and relaxation for teachers often stressed by the day. These lounges are often neglected by school designers and builders with budget limitations. These programs are modest but highly visible and appreciated by an important California Casualty segment. The programs also promotes to employees a culture friendly to societal programs.

Look to Suppliers. Helping suppliers makes sense in part because they are a key stakeholder and crucial to a business strategy. When those suppliers and their workers are in developing countries, active assistance from a global organization can be especially impactful.

There are a host of food brands that have developed programs to help farmers and other suppliers in developing countries improve their methods to become better stewards of the land and gain better yields as well. The Cadbury Cocoa Partnership, which was founded in Ghana in 2008, for example, helps farmers and their communities with knowledge and skills around sustainable farming, business management, child labor issues, increasing net income from farming and other sources, and women appreciation. The goal is to solidify the source of cocoa, improve farmer livelihoods, strengthen communities, and inspire the next generation of cocoa farmers.

Technology and Innovation. Much of the increase in disruption has come from the digital world involving IofT (Internet of Things), data analytics, the Internet and e-commerce, and these can be applied as well in societal programs. The Grameen Foundation, for example, has blended technology, digital platforms, and a trusted human network to allow the world's poor, especially women, self-reliance in financial transaction even without Internet access, a smartphone, or even the ability to read. They can pay bills, save money, get loans, transfer money without going to a bank, and access information that can help them make health decisions, farm better, and more. Among their partners is Wells Fargo Bank, for whom this is a natural alliance.

Enhance an Existing Program. An ideal candidate for a signature social program may be hidden in plain sight, performing marginally and receiving limited visibility. That was the case with the hand-washing program at Lifebuoy, as told in Chapter 2, that had been alive for over a century. In 2013, it was enhanced with new resources, a formalized program centered around schools, vivid emotional videos about its success in three villages, a decision to scale to many countries, and, importantly, a brand, "Help a Child Reach 5."

Firms tend to avoid external programs lacking polish and containing flaws. But such a nonprofit, if it has a promising purpose or mission and program, with resources and some innovation, could quickly become an impact player. It is ironic that on the business side, buying small promising firms to fill in gaps is a familiar and often strategically successful strategy. There is no reason that firms looking for an external nonprofit partner can't search for "bargains." They can look for a program that is struggling because it lacks the resources to finetune the offering or to promote effectively. A firm could then energize the partner, make an impact on a societal need, and own a signature program relationship. In contrast, a firm might have less to offer to a winning nonprofit with a strong brand or find it difficult to create an ownable relationship niche.

The Firm's Heritage, Assets/Expertise, & Offering

One goal is to find signature social programs that go beyond having a comfortable fit with the firm by linking it to the customer base or the interests of the employees. Another is to draw on its heritage and thus its values and culture, its assets, and its offering.

Heritage. Some organizations are blessed with heritage of a social purpose or mission and associated programs that may have been articulated by the founder or another firm employee decades earlier. A return to these roots can crystallize or energize a culture and program that that may have weathered or faded.

Lifebuoy has a heritage of making soap that cleans while attacking germs that dates back to its founding in the 1880s to be a hygiene product relevant to a pandemic of the day. That heritage supports the authenticity of the "Help a Child Reach 5" program. Salesforce was founded with the 1-1-1 (now Pledge 1%) program embedded into it. Patagonia has an environmental purpose that was part of its DNA when Yvon Chouinard, a mountain climber, surfer, and environmentalist, founded Patagonia in 1973 to forge environmentally friendly climbing pitons out of scrap metal.

Assets and expertise. Look at your organization's assets and expertise. How can they be employed to create a signature social program? What really fits? The Goldman initiatives described in Chapter 6 all drew on the organization's expertise, its entrepreneurial customer base, and its financial strength. Many of the sponsors of Habitat for Humanity make appliances or building materials that go into homes and thus have products and expertise to contribute to Habitat.

Going beyond your expertise can be risky. Domestor, an Unilever premium disinfectant brand, took on the job of improving access to clean, safe toilets knowing that over 2 billion people lack such an access. The effort started in 2009 with a program to design and build clean, safe toilets that turned out to be beyond their expertise, so they pivoted to two other programs. One, that leveraged their product and distribution assets, was a new toilet cleaning powder that sold for 2 cents in a single use packet, making enough money to cover costs. The second, launched in South Africa, was a program to teach school janitors how to properly clean toilets, support them with cleaning products and equipment, and teach children about toilet use.[64]

The Offering. One way to leverage assets and skills is to draw on offerings or their application. The offering can be embedded in the programs. Lifebuoy applied its products and expertise around its "Help a Child Reach 5" handwashing program. Reliance's financial arm adapted its lending programs to villages in India. Tesla provides energy savings when people switch to electric cars. Lego provides their product to support programs to give needy kids the game tools that they could not afford.

Discovery Limited, one of South Africa's leading health insurers, launched its vitality programs that rewards customers with lower premiums if they adopt healthful habits. Their efforts are screened though Vitality health check, which tracks health indicators like blood pressure, cholesterol levels, and BMI (body mass index), with measures of exercise and smoking frequency. One result— customers have changed their behavior and improved their health, resulting in a Discovery-connected health cost savings of over $1.2 billion from 2008 to 2018.[65]

A program can also be based on improving the societal impact of their products. PepsiCo took that route under the branded initiative "Winning with Purpose" under Indra Nooyi when she became PepsiCo CEO in 2006.[66] There was widespread skepticism about redirection from the maker of sodas and Frito-Lay snacks. But Nooyi had the perspective, talent, and strategy credentials to make it happen. The effort involved a host of programs. Two were involved in changing food products to make them healthier but still appealing. The result was:

- **Product upgrades**. Existing products were upgraded to create "Better for You" options by reducing sugar, salt, saturated fat, and unhealthy additives. For example, in 2020, 48% of the beverage portfolio had 100 Calories or less from added sugars per 12 ounce serving, an improvement of 8% over the prior three years and moving toward a goal of 67% by 2025.

- **Adding "Good for You" product lines**. PepsiCo has added plant-based options with a sustainable value proposition through brands like Quaker, Off the Eaten Path, Sabra, Alvalle, Naked Juice, Bare, and Health Warrior. A joint venture with Beyond Meat, the PLANeT Partnership, was designed to develop, produce, and market innovative snack and beverage products made from plant-based protein. "Good for the planet" product delivery platforms like SodaStream and SodaStream Professional offered access to drink products without single-use packaging.

When Nooyi stepped down 14 years later, sales had increased 80%, the stock price doubled, and much of the "purpose" program had shown tangible economic and social results.

Criteria in Selecting the Right Program

Whether there is an active search for a social program that will merit signature status, it is necessary to know what a potential winner might look like. What are the criteria that should be employed to screen and evaluate? Three stand out. A potentially impactful signature social program will:

- **Inspire** (answers the "why" question). The target societal need or issue should be feel real and engender empathy along with an emotional response. It needs to matter and inspire, not only to activate employees and partners, but also to accentuate the potential to help the image of the sponsoring business brands.

- **Be credible** (answers the "how" question). The program concept should be convincing with an approach that is innovative and clever without an "already seen that" impression. There should be access to the assets, skills, and resources needed to move the needle, be visible, and create an authentic commitment by the stakeholders. It cannot be perceived as lofty goals unlikely to happen or worse, empty words or self-serving braggadocio.

- **Fit the sponsoring business**. Long-term success is more probable if the signature program is integrated with a business. Integration is made easier if the signature social program fits the sponsoring business or firm; is consistent with its culture, values, and people; and can enhance the visibility, image, and loyalty of a business brand without reducing its authenticity and trust. A fit doesn't need to be directly tied to a business but could involve, for example, a commitment and active partner in an annual fund-raising event.

Programs Evolve

As the program options appear and develop, they need to be screened. However, there is a complication. Societal programs evolve. They do not arrive as full-grown adults or even close to that stage. The initial program will need modification involving creative thinking and innovation investments in order to advance to signature status. There are few successful programs that did not start small and evolve substantially.

One implication is that screening needs to imagine the upside possibilities and forecast the innovation and investment that will be required. Some of the most successful offerings were almost killed because there was a problem that, given current technology or infrastructure, seemed like a fatal limitation. But persistence, a faith in innovation, and an eye on the upside resulted in a winner.

Another implication is that investing in an embryonic and defective idea may seem unwise, but it might also turn out to be the basis of a program that becomes impactful in multiple ways. Recall Prophet's PFNP program that was limited and flawed but led to a group of programs that together had a magnified impact. Creative thinking, new insights, and focused refinement, enhancement, and adaptation can turn a weak appearing idea into a solid winner.

Programs evolve, but it is not helpful to wait until the program or a program enhancement is perfect. A better strategy is to try them out and put them out there. Plan to observe, learn, and modify. Let the evolution process work. You learn by doing, by getting close to the societal problem and those affected. It is a surety that improvement will occur, and it is probable that the result will be game changing.

We now turn to another imperative: use the signature social program to enhance a business brand as well as impact the societal challenge.

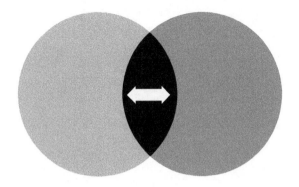

Part III
Integrating the Signature Social Program into the Business

Integrating a signature program into a business provides a supportive home, protecting the program from the risks and vulnerabilities of being by itself. It involves the signature program supporting and receiving support from a business partner. Chapter 8 discusses how a program can help a business by enhancing its brand, a role that has not been well understood or recognized in part because it has not be tied to a structured view of the brand equity of the partner business. Chapter 9 is about how the firm can help the program if the integration is working by being an active partner providing an endorsement and access to resources. It also discusses how two organizations can blend, a task especially challenging if the signature program is an external nonprofit.

Chapter 8

INTEGRATION: THE SIGNATURE SOCIAL PROGRAM JOB 2: ENHANCE A BUSINESS

The primary focus of your brand message must be on how special you are.

Larry Light, Brand Strategist

Barclays Gains Trust

The Barclays brand had a trust problem in 2011 because of their perceived role in the manipulation of interest rates that was blamed as a contributor to the 2008 financial meltdown.[67] It is not a stretch to conclude that Barclays then was the least trusted brand in the least trusted sector in the UK. Barclays decided to change and in February of 2013, it announced a new brand mission: "Helping people achieve their ambitions—in the right way" and encouraged the 140,000-employee team to create supporting programs that would fit.

The newly empowered and inspired Barclays employee team created over 40 responsive social programs. Four of these were combined to form the Digital Eagles with a mission to teach the public, particularly the elderly and kids, about thriving in the digital world. Starting with 17 employees, it eventually grew to involve over 17,000, Among its programs were informal Tea and Teach sessions about digital coping that were held in the branches on weekends, and Digital Wings, an online series of courses that advanced people from newbies to confident users.

In June 2014, the existing descriptive communication about why the "changed" Barclays should be trusted was replaced with real stories of real people around employee programs presented in commercials and videos. One of the Digital Eagle stories told of Steve Rich, who had lost his ability to play football (soccer to Americans) because of a car accident but grew to love "walking football"—usually played with six to a team on a small field with no running— and again experience the joy of the sport. Wanting to help others do the same, he decided to raise awareness of walking football and turn it into a nationwide game in Britain.

With the help of Digital Eagles, Rich created a website that connected individual players with some 400 active teams and facilitated the scheduling of games and formation of leagues. It also helped Rich and others get in touch with some former football mates. The viewers of the video version of the story got to know Rich and his wife and grandson, see him reenergized by the game, experience his interaction with a Digital Eagle, and feel the exhilaration and pride in what he had done. His efforts were partly responsible for the growing interest in the sport and the formation of a national tournament.

These stories precipitated changes in the perception of Barclays and inspired and energized customers and prospective customers.[68] Less than two years from the start of the campaign in summer 2014, trust was up 33 percent, consideration was up 130 percent, emotional connection was up 35 percent (versus 5 percent for the category average) and "reassurance that your finances are secure" was up 46 percent. The new campaign drove six times as much change in trust and five times as much change in consideration as the description of a "changed Barclays" campaign that preceded it. Further, Barclays received 5,000 positive mentions in the press, a sharp change from the relentless negative press that they had previously endured. And it was a signature social program that was well-presented and solidly linked to Barclay's that did it. The Barclays image and connection with people experienced a dramatic change.

The Barclays story illustrates the power of integration. How the societal effort and the Digital Eagles signature program, in particularly, were enabled and funded by a business in crisis and how the signature programs ended up becoming an ongoing "solution" to their external image and employee morale.

The signature social program, whether internal or an external nonprofit, should not be isolated from a sponsoring firm. It should not be on ongoing drag on the resources of the firm. Instead it will an active partner and teammate not only impacting a societal need by also adding value to a business and, in turn, receive an endorsement and access to resources from that firm. There will be a win-win partnership. The purpose, the vision, and the position should be intertwined. The staff should have a working relationship within the firm for an internal signature program and across organization for an external nonprofit signature program. That is the goal.

The glue of the integration process is the symbiotic relationship between a business and its adopted partner, a signature social program. Each will materially help the other.

- A signature social program can affirm the purpose and culture of a business partner and lift its energy, image and connection with employees and other stakeholders. It can provide respect, admiration, pride and even inspiration. Any business needs such an enhancement and some with mature functional offerings may be desperate for it. This role works for an external nonprofit that has been adopted by a business as well as an internal program.

- A business, as a strategic partner, can materially help the social program whether it is internal or external. It can provide credibility and commitment by its endorsement, image traits not easily obtained. As a partner, it can also provide a steady flow of financial support and access to resources including its expertise, marketing budget, employee volunteers, market insights, customer base and more.

An evaluation of the signature social program that fails to consider all the ways that it creates value may make the strategic mistake of undervaluing a program or exaggerating its weakness. This chapter will focus on the signature program helping a business partner. Chapter 9 will turn to the other side of the integration, how the firm can help the signature program and how the integration of two organizations can be managed.

Why Add Economic Value to a Business?

The primary job, Job 1, of the signature social program is to make a meaningful difference in a set of societal problems or issues that feel important.

There is also a Job 2, a secondary but important role, to add economic value to a sponsoring business, usually by enhancing the brand of the sponsoring business—internally to inspire its employees or externally to provide a point of connection for customers, suppliers, investors, and other stakeholders. There are other ways to add value. An energy reduction program could affect costs meaningfully, for example, but even in that case, helping the sponsoring brand is usually an important benefit as well.

Adding value to a business is part of the glue that makes the integration of the signature social program into a business possible. It motivates a business to asset the signature program because it is clear that the more success it has in doing so the more brand benefits will be received. The results is more and better access to its resources and more reliable long-term financial commitment. This companion value-add from the business to the signature program is the other glue element that will be discussed further in the chapter that follows.

Adding value to a business may not seem appropriate because people who "do good" do not typically look for personal advantage nor do they brag about it. If the "adding value" role is mishandled and appears to be the more important program rationale, the authenticity of the program is at risk. More on this issue later in the chapter. This Job 2 role is a game changer for both the signature social programs and for the sponsoring firm or business and has gained widespread acceptance. In some circumstances it can be a critical business success factor.

There are three reasons why it is important that a signature social program should take on the goal of adding economic value to a business.

1. A Signature Social Program is Uniquely Able to Enhance a Brand

A signature social program should enhance a brand because it is uniquely suited to do so. It is likely to attract attention and get remembered because it is relatable, intriguing, and inspiring. Further, it can illicit feelings of warmth, pride, and likability plus deliver self-expressive benefits, all of which can influence the image of a business brand and its relationship to stakeholders. The power of a signature social program to affect a business brand is especially important for the many businesses that have offerings that realistically are functional and mundane. A signature program can make the most boring brand become interesting.

The signature social program is also a powerful communication vehicle because of its focus, impact, and its brand. In contrast, communicating an overall societal effort is almost impossible because it involves fragmented grant programs, volunteering, and unbranded energy reduction goals. All are difficult to communicate and can be perceived as being exaggerated, self-serving and lacking in distinctiveness.

Enhancing the brand equity of the business brand almost always has an impact on most stakeholders. Dove's Self-Esteem Program from Chapter 2, for example, can instill pride in the Dove brand, which in turn can affect the Dove customers and employees as well as other stakeholders. The impact of a social program at Barclays created a quantitatively dramatic improvement in the Barclays brand, which was living under a very negative cloud. The 10,000 Women program, introduced in Chapter 6, certainly helped the Goldman brand by showing how its skills, get-the-job done innovation, and relationships can be leveraged for good.

2. It is a Competitive Necessity

There is momentum to address societal problems and issues in nearly all markets. As a result, firms are creating new social programs or energizing and expanding existing ones. The reality that competitors are on the move represents a threat and an opportunity. There is a significant penalty to be regarded as disinterested or deficient in addressing societal challenges and a huge advantage to be a committed participant and an industry social program leader. Doing nothing is not an option as more and more firms enter the fray and up their game.

The forces behind this momentum are documented in Chapter 4. The traditional shareholder model of business has been replaced by a stakeholder model. There is a significant group of employees, customers, investors, and other stakeholders that are developing perceptions and making decisions based on the perceived social effort of a firm. Add the visibility of major societal problems and issues and include the realization that firms and business have resources, management skills, and strategic agility that can make them effective contributors in this arena. Plus the need for some brands for energy and image lift that, for them, only visible signature social programs can deliver.

Enabling this trend is an emerging belief that it is acceptable for social programs to add economic value to a business as well as impact a societal need. That once unpopular idea has been advanced by thought leaders, management theorists, the ascension of the "stakeholder" economic paradigm, and hundreds of books with titles like "Do Good: Embracing Brand Citizenship to Fuel Both Purpose and Profit." That means that those firms that fall behind in the societal area will have an economic deficit to overcome.

One of many influencers was the British social issue writer, John Elkington, who in 1994 coined the phrase, "triple bottom line" to represent a business that succeeded in being profitable while still making a social contribution.[69] It explicitly enunciated that a goal for business doesn't need to sacrifice profits if it elects to do social good.

An important addition to the discussion was a seminal HBR article in early 2011, in which Michael Porter and Mark Kramer argued that we need to reinvent capitalism by having businesses create signature social programs (although they used different terms) that provide value to society AND economic value to the firm, "shared value" in their terminology. The integration of signature social programs into the business is, as they observe, a very different motivation than social responsibility (do the right thing) or philanthropy (share your profits with "feel good" contributions). This shared value concept elevated the concept of a signature social program adding economic value, in part because it had the imprint of the most influential business strategy thought leader of the day, Michael Porter. It was no longer a side benefit that occasionally appeared.

3 The Signature Social Program Will Gain Support

For signature social programs, having a sponsoring firm or business partner that benefits economically from the relationship is strategically critical whether the program is internal or a nonprofit external to the firm. The sponsoring firm or business provides long-term financial support, access to assets and expertise, and the endorsement of a credible firm or business. It is the other half of the symbiotic relationship. As noted above, a business is encouraged to support a signature program because that will increase the benefit it receives. Again Chapter 9 will discuss this side of the integration opportunity.

What elements of a business brand can, and should, a signature social program attempt to influence?

How a Signature Social Program Can Enhance a Business Brand

The exploration starts with the three dimensions of the brand equity of a business brand—brand visibility and energy, brand image, and brand loyalty. Each of these have components that are especially suitable for a signature social program to influence. They will provide a starting point for those seeking a way for a social program to make a difference not only on a societal challenge, but also on business performance.

Brand Visibility & Energy

A brand that is visible has a huge advantage. It is more likely to be considered when a person or organization has an application for which the brand should be relevant. An unknown brand will likely be on the sidelines. Visibility also leads to a perception of competence and quality based on the potentially unconscious belief that if you heard of it, there must be a reason, it must have enjoyed market acceptance.

Brand energy is a route to visibility and more. It means that innovation is thriving, the marketplace is excited, things are happening, and there are reasons to talk about the brand. Nearly all brands, including new brands needing momentum or mature brands fighting off irrelevance and stagnation, need more energy. That is especially true for established leader brands with products and applications that are not interesting or newsworthy and may even be boring—think of a packaged pudding or decades old software. Audience members have better things to do than consider benefits or even innovations in categories with a brand they take for granted.

While an offering may be boring, mundane, and uninvolving, its signature social program around an inspiring purpose or mission can create energy and visibility that can come from several sources. The social or environmental problem or its innovative solution may generate interest that the offering lacks. Recall the case of Unilever brands in Chapter 2. Dove's Evolution campaign showing the effort that goes behind creating what is an "artificial model look" got over 100 million YouTube views and created unpaid exposure estimated to be worth over $150 million. And the bar soap Lifebuoy, developed three videos around its "Help a Child Reach 5" hand washing programs that got over 45 million views. Those both contained a lot of visibility and energy for rather mundane products. In both cases, it was the signature programs that got awareness and energy that would not have been possible by focusing only on their products.

Brand Image

The brand image is a core piece of any brand's equity. It is what comes to mind when confronted with the brand. The image can include a host of perceptions, feelings, imagery, and connections. The addition of a visible signature social program to the business brand can add to its image, reinforce something that is already there, or neutralize a negative perception. It can, for example:

Represent a point of difference, which can be a meaningful asset. A signature social program such as Dove's Self-Esteem, for example, will be unique to the Dove brand and thus distinguish it from other brands, especially those that exist only with a "me-too" functional benefit. The Salesforce's Pledge 1% (formerly 1-1-1) program is "owned" by Salesforce and has been adopted by over 10,000 firms. For those firms especially, Salesforce is the recognized founder and exemplar for the program and gets credit for a leadership role in a meaningful movement by the "members" and others that are aware of the program and might aspire to join.

Be memorable, a key communication goal. The signature program will stand out among the other dozens of brand attributes in part because there is admiration and an emotional response rarely seen when functional benefits are the focus. Skepticism and counter arguing seldom arise when a social program is being discussed because there is the ability to engage and focus on a societal need that feels real.

Combat negative publicity. Bad things happen even when your firm has done nothing wrong. Negative press can emerge in part because, as our own insight plus hundreds of studies confirm, negative news is more salable than positive news. Correcting the resulting image is difficult because any argument can attract attention to it, making the situation worse. A signature social program with prestigious supporters, some perhaps part of a board of advisors, provide a way out. It can change the discussion away from the negative and stimulate credible spokespeople to say "yes, but…" Barclays is a case in point.

Providing credibility to a social purpose or mission. Such a purpose or mission can be difficult to communicate because there may be an assumption that it is just words and not deeds. The signature social brand provides substance that offers proof points in the form of program details, success measures, and personal stories. Substance delivers credibility to the total societal effort.

Providing a growth platform. A signature social program can create admired characteristics and self-expressive benefits that can support a product or service. Green products such as Mentor, organic products from Whole Foods, or healthier snacks from Pepsico all have stimulated growth based on their positioning. In this case, the firm is both the business brand and the signature social brand. Mars Petcare, for instance, expanded its mission from pet food into a more holistic view of pet care and into the larger ecosystem of pet health, a societal need. Growth platforms emerged when the firm developed advances in nutrition and provided high-quality medical care with over 2,000 veterinarian pet hospitals.

Position the brand and frame the discussion. By making the signature social brand visible, it can make the societal challenge and resulting program a part of any discussion or decision involving the business brand. It can potentially create a new subcategory in which offerings that lack a societal dimension are not preferred or even considered.

Engender trust. The entry of a social program reflects values that are compatible with the perception of honesty, authenticity, and ultimately trust, one of the most important elements of a brand, especially a brand in a service or b-to-b space. If you have trust, you are respected and if you lose trust, it is difficult to get it back. The Edelman Trust Barometer, in which trust has been measured for two decades in over 26 countries, has documented the power of trust.[70] Trust is just behind price and quality with respect to purchase criterion, a finding that holds true across geography, gender, and age groups. It is also a strong predicter of recommending or defending the brand. The Barclays story dramatically shows how a signature social program can affect the visibility and trust image of a sponsor business brand.

Brand Loyalty

Brand loyalty is at the heart of any brand's value because once obtained, loyalty is persistent. Customer inertia will benefit the business brand that has earned loyalty. Breaking a loyalty link is difficult and expensive for a competitor. As such, one brand-building goal is to strengthen the size and intensity of each loyalty segment by making the basis of the customer relationship consistent over time and, whenever possible, rich, deep, and meaningful.

A signature social program can elevate the attitude toward the sponsoring business brand and increase the intensity of loyalty to the business brand in several ways. It can provide perceptions of:

Brand affinity. One driver of loyalty is simply liking a brand, created when a brand is associated with something like a person, a program, or an outcome that is well liked. This concept, which psychologists call affect (liking) transfer, is supported by a huge volume of theoretical and experimental evidence, in part based on the need for cognitive and emotional consistency. There is an uncomfortable inconsistency when a person has a liking for one entity (a signature program) and not for a closely associated entity (the sponsoring firm or business). There will be pressure to resolve the inconsistency by adjusting the liking of one or the other.

Making a signature social program such as Lifebuoy's "Help a Child Reach 5" (that is addressing the tragic fact that "2 million kids die before they reach 5") visible with emotional, involved stories can evoke a positive liking response to the program, its components and its outcomes, and even the characters in the stories. This liking can then get transferred to the Lifebuoy brand. The brand is seen as emanating from an organization that cares and is concerned with societal need challenges, not only about their bottom line.

There are levels of affect. The ultimate connection will come when a signature social brand is not only liked, but inspires, and this feeling becomes part of the business brand. Employees and customers that experience this inspiration will be at a higher loyalty level.

Affinity in addition to providing ongoing preference also affects perceptions. People, it turns out, filter or distort information that runs counter to their beliefs and feelings. Thus, affinity for Salesforce will make it harder for competitors to argue their superiority with facts and descriptions of offerings.

Brand affinity affected by a signature social program need not have a broad reach. Even if a customer segment size involved may seem relatively small, it can still mean the difference between struggling and enjoying financial success. It can also affect the most important customers, which might be few in number, but huge in influence and impact.

California Casually, an auto and home insurance company introduced in Chapter 7, services groups among the largest of which are educators and highway patrol organizations. The firm joined with these two groups to become a founding member of Impact Teen Driving which develops, promotes, and facilitates evidence-based education to stop the reckless and distracted driving that leads to the number one cause of teen deaths in the U.S. This initiative showed a shared concern about teen accidents and led to a deeper relationship with these key customer groups.

Shared Values. A signature social program can create or support a shared values bond between the brand and stakeholders. An important and growing segment of all stakeholders wants a brand relationship that is based on or includes meaningful programs that address societal challenges, because such programs represent their values. When the shared values are strong, these customers impact the marketplace with their loyalty and support. Such a bond is difficult for a competitor to break.

Self-expressive benefits. Being associated with a brand's signature social program can provide self-expressive benefits by affirming a person's values and passions. Using a Dove product is a way to express a set of values and personality that resonates with their self-esteem programs. Being a volunteer for a Food Bank indicates your empathy for those that are homeless or have food deficit.

Brand communities. Becoming part of a signature social program brand community (a group that shares an interest area or activity) represents a high level of involvement and can create a special relationship that will enhance loyalty. The HOGs, the Harley Davidson Owners Group, is the prototypical example as is the Susan G. Komen 3-Day walk for breast cancer. Both involve participates and supporters that share tips, news about events, and their emotional highs with fellow members. The result is an intense level of affinity, shared values, self-expressive benefits, and loyalty toward a brand which becomes an active part of the membership. Chapter 12 elaborates.

Communicating and Linking the Signature Social Program

The signature program needs to be communicated to enhance a business brand. It is no time for false modesty. The importance of the societal need, the impact the program will make on that need, and why the program is unique and credible needs to be told. The target stakeholders need to be identified and a wide variety of communication tools should be considered, including program events, social vehicles, and the use of stories that engender an emotional understanding of program impact.

An important communication goal is to create a link between the signature social programs and the sponsoring brand. The link can come from a persistent and prominent endorsement, from joint activities and events, and many other forms. The end task is to make sure that when the brand is mentioned, the signature social program comes to mind.

The signature program may also have the task of helping not only its sponsoring brand, such as Lifebuoy, but also brands above it in the vertical brand chain, which could involve different audiences and linking efforts. The Unilever firm brand plus the Unilever Compass (formerly USLP) Brand and the Sustainable Living Brand all get "proof points" and energy from the "Help a Child Reach 5" program. The brand linking effort does not have to reach a broad audience, but rather those stakeholders, including employees, investors, and social influencers who will be influenced by having the image of these three brands enhanced or reinforced.

Quantifying the Impact on Brand Equity

It is often a challenge to quantify the change of a brand's visibility, image, or loyalty on financial performance. Like any intangible, the link to performance is complex especially when the impact is spread out years into the future. So how to proceed?

Conceptually. The best approach can be to construct a conceptual model of the business strategy and what is critical to its success. The model should consider the relative long-term impact of a social program-driven change in brand equity on success factors such as the performance of employees, the attraction of customers, and the affinity of other stakeholders such as investors. The impact importance should become clear even if numbers are not available. Quantifying the value of an intangible such as people, culture, or processes is virtually impossible and brand equity is in that category. There are too many causal factors that the absence of any one of them would often mean failure.

Case studies. There is no shortage of role models within and outside a firm. These case studies are "quasi-experiments," they have a before-treatment-after design with the presumption that the difference between the after and before is likely due to the treatment. Barclays is one such case. Many others, described in this book, demonstrate that it can be done, that signature social programs are conducted that enhance rather that harm profitability.

Long-term perspective. The impact of a signature social program on both brand equity and business performance is likely to extend over years. The need is thus to create measures that reflect that long-term impact. One vehicle is the long-term value of a customer, based on the likely profit flow over many years which will vary by loyalty levels. Thus, measures of the number of customers affected by a change in brand equity segmented by loyalty can represent the long-term impact far better than short term financials.

Empirical analysis can buttress the argument. Elements of brand equity like visibility, image, or loyalty, can be measured in a tracking survey and linked to financial measures. There are two qualifications. As noted, it is easy to use short-term financials as they are available, but that is rarely the relevant goal. Second, rather than relying on the correlation between brand equity and performance, it is important to look at the impact of brand equity changes on performance in order to avoid direction of causation issues. The best analysis, of course, will be based on experimental data that can control for many external forces and can find a surrogate measures for long-term impacts.

Brand Equity Does Pay Off

If a signature social programs can enhance brand equity, do we have any evidence that brand equity changes impact the business? Actually, we do. Besides the myriad of case studies that illustrate this, there are empirical studies that show that, on average, positive changes in indicators of brand equity do affect financial performance as reflected in stock market reaction.

Two studies by Robert Jacobson and myself show a causal link from brand equity to stock return.[71] In both, the model controls for the direction of causation in part by analyzing the impact of a change in brand equity on future stock return while controlling for variables like advertising and management quality.

The first is based on an annual perceived quality rating (which is highly correlated with other brand equity measures) for 34 U.S. brands who have the bulk of their sales under the firm brand. The second uses brand equity, measured by the percent favorable toward a brand, less the percent unfavorable (also correlated with other brand equity dimensions), and involves quarterly data from nine high tech firms over an eight-year period, resulting in 250 observations. In both studies, brand equity had a significant impact on stock return. The impact was nearly as high as that of accounting ROI, which is a well-known driver of stock return.

Another study by Michigan researchers, Claes Fornell and colleagues, used a customer satisfaction brand equity measure based on the American Customer Satisfaction Index (ACSI).[72] With over 600 data points over nine years, they found that an increase in the index of 1% would drive a change in stock return of 4.6%, and a portfolio of stocks in the top 20% with their ACSI score had a return double that of the S&P 1000.

We also know that brands have been estimated to be worth between 15 and 20% of their value for brands like Nike, Apple, Toyota, and GE to well over 50% for Coca-Cola (including all their brands), McDonald's, and BMV. This comes from the brand evaluation done each year by Interbrand, in which a subjective analysis is used to apportion the influence of a brand among other intangible assets.[73]

Similar findings emerge when brand equity is based on employee satisfaction, as reflected in Fortune's list of 100 Best Companies to Work for in America. Eligible companies must have over 1,000 employees and be scored by a sixty-question employee survey around trust, leadership, culture, and values. Using data that spanned 26 years, the future stock return (the change in stock price during the following year plus dividends) of those on the top 100 list were compared to their industry peers. The result, those 100 Best Companies outperformed their peers by from 2.3 to 3.8% per year over a 28-year period.[74] That is 90% to 180% cumulative difference in return. The research was extended to thirteen countries and in nine of them, the results were even higher than those found in the U.S. data.[75]

Walking a Fine Line

There needs to be a sensitivity to the charge that a firm's desire to help a business by improving its visibility, image, and customer loyalty is the primary, and maybe the only goal rather than being part of Job 2. In fact, there can be the suspicion, internally as well as externally, that a firm may exaggerate their societal effort or even make it up in order to create good press, that the firm is motivated to create these programs only to improve their brand rather than to improve lives. There is a delicate balance between having a business benefit from an effective signature social program and avoiding the appearance of being shallow, self-centered, and crassly commercial.

To avoid the wrong impression about motivation, a real passion and commitment to the signature social program should be in evidence. If there is no authentic passion, no heart, then it is unlikely that the program will be effective or long-lived, whatever boost it might give a business in the short run. And perhaps worse, it can lead stakeholders and others to conclude that the firm's social effort is insincere, an effort to look good with an exaggerated program, and probably ill-conceived with little commitment or impact. That would undercut the ability of the program to help the brand and ultimately risk significant brand damage.

This challenge is greatest when there is not a natural fit within the firm and the signature program. Lifebuoy's heritage of using hygiene to fight disease and the fact that their main product is soap, provided credibility for their motivation for "Help a Child Reach 5." While the Dove offering and business had little connection with any self-esteem program, it still found ways to make its program fit. People are comfortable with the Dove association because of its long-term commitment and how the program evolved and engaged.

The question is how to demonstrate real passion and commitment, as Dove did, while still helping a business. It starts, of course, with authentically having passion and commitment as demonstrated by:

- **Making the program an integral part of the business brand** and its strategy and not an appendage. If the signature social program both represents and is represented by the organizational purpose/mission, values, assets, and energy, the risk especially with employees will be greatly reduced.

- **Employee engagement** will signal authentic commitment internally and sometimes externally as well. The engagement level is enhanced when the signature social program becomes part of the culture, most employees understand the program, and it becomes a part of their professional and even personal lives.

- **A long-term meaningful commitment** year after year says loudly that there is an authentic and passionate belief in the societal need. One commitment signal is a visible endorsement with an annual fundraising event. Another is ongoing initiatives, improvements, and expansions showing that the signature program is not just coasting. Still another is to demonstrate, perhaps by accepting the Pledge 1% challenge, that the business societal investment is meaningful, given the size and resources of the firm.

- **Be an involved thought leader**. Host conferences about the issues, have a website or a place on the business website to discuss problems and solutions, or create a brand community around the issue, as Patagonia (discussed in Chapter 11) has around elements of the environment. Be generally seen as being more than just a program.

In Chapter 9, we turn to the other half of the integration clue, the motivation and ability of a business to help a signature program.

Chapter 9

INTEGRATION—THE BUSINESS SUPPORTS THE SIGNATURE PROGRAM

One of the most important things you can do on this earth is to let people know they are not alone.
Shannon L. Alder, American author

Habitat for Humanity—The Best at Creating Business Partners

Habitat for Humanity begin when Millard and Linda Fuller had the idea of partnership housing, where those in need would work beside volunteers to build affordable homes that would be partially financed by fundraising. After trying out the concept in Georgia and then Africa, they founded Habitat for Humanity in 1976. Its current mission, "seeking to put God's love into action, bringing people together to build homes, communities and hope." reflects its heritage.

Four years later, Habitat had built 340 homes in seven countries. By 2020, it had helped more that 30 million people have homes that were newly built or restored. They were doing so around the world at a pace of affecting over seven million people each year, over 95 percent outside the U.S., with a volunteer effort that exceeded 1.4 million people.

Habitat has expanded their offering over time. Some examples. In 1991 it added the Habitat Restore home improvement stores and donation centers selling new and gently used furniture, appliances, home goods, building materials and more. In 2009, Habitat unveiled the Build Louder public policy advocacy campaign, which focuses on neighborhood revitalization and secure tenure policies. In 2017, Habitat introduced the Quality of Life Framework to support efforts to upgrade neighborhoods, because having a safe, stable, and vibrant neighborhood is a springboard to opportunity.

Habitat is one of the best at finding active firm partners. It has over 100 sponsors, 20 of which are legacy sponsors who pledge over $1 million a year on an ongoing basis making rolling five-year commitments. Two legacy sponsors, ABBIE and Thrivent, contribute over $10 million each year. Of this group of 20, two have been partners for over 35 years, and 16 for over eight years. An additional 70 firms have made long-term commitments that involved smaller amounts but include volunteer support. Over 20 firms engage in cause marketing providing vehicles for their customers to support Habitat. Charity Miles, for example, an iPhone and Android app, donates to Habitat for every mile a user covers by walking, running, or biking. Delta SkyMiles allows members to donate miles to Habitat through the Delta Air Lines SkyWish program.

Why was Habitat so successful at developing this team of sponsoring firms who have integrated Habitat into their strategies and cultures. Among the reasons:

- **A strong brand**. Habitat's brand strength comes from its storied heritage, celebrity participation (President Carter's volunteering has been well-publicized), serving a visible need, the endorsement and visibility created by its sponsors, and being so good at what it does. From concept to the last nail, Habitat is competent at delivering on its promise. However, there is also an emotional attraction. People feel pride in visualizing volunteers building or repairing structures, a family gaining home ownership, and a neighborhood flourishing.

- **An employee volunteer outlet**. Habitat provides a branded outlet for employee volunteering that is painless to use and rewards with worthwhile projects which can take place in exotic, eye-opening locales in far off countries. Involvement is made convenient with guidance as to what options are available and how to proceed.

- **Ownable options**. It provides ways to carve out areas that a sponsor can own. Home Depot, as noted, has focused on homes for veterans, AbbVie carved out hurricane rebuilding, and Wells Fargo, the financing of home building. Thrivent has provided over six million volunteer hours from employees and clients under a co-brand "Faith Builds."

- **Fits with building products**. Habitat leverages a natural fit with firms that are involved with building. Yale supplies locks, Whirlpool provides appliances, Schneider Electric gives electrical equipment, GAF provides roofing materials, MaxLite supplies lighting products, etc. Some donations are made at cost but, more importantly, there is a strong link to the firm's business and their sponsorship. But it is not the case that such a fit is necessary, AbbVie, a medicine firm introduced in Chapter 7, and Thrivent, a financial services firm, had no such connection.

Firms are now motivated to create or improve efforts to address societal needs and issues. They want to make a difference while helping business brands in the process. To move in that direction, it is imperative that the signature social program and brand not only be created but become strong. It should have energy and visibility, an image that instills respect and admiration, and an active set of stakeholder communities.

How do you build a strong signature social program? A productive route will be to make sure that the sponsoring business becomes an active partner that will provide resources, credibility, and visibility. From the viewpoint of a signature program, the need is to find and activate a business partner. If the signature program is internal, the sponsor could be an internal firm or business that is benefiting by the association. The challenge may be to make the business organization informed, supported, and active. If the signature brand is an external nonprofit, the sponsor could be a firm or business that has adopted it. The Habitat for Humanity story shows how powerful locating and nurturing sponsor firms or businesses can be. The challenge now includes finding and motivating a business partner.

Find and Activate a Business Partner

For signature social programs, having a sponsoring partner that benefits economically from the relationship is strategically critical, whether the social program is internal or a nonprofit external to the firm. It is part of the glue that enables the integration of the signature program into the business. The other part, the value of the signature program to the business, was the subject of the last chapter.

The sponsoring partner provides three value-adds to the signature social program that can fuel its long-term success and sometimes even its survival. It is a win-win.

First, a sponsorship is the basis for long-term ongoing support. When the signature social program, whether internal or external, is considered a dead drain on the business drawing resources from needed strategic investments and effective tactical programs, the long-term commitment to the programs will be at risk, particularly when a business experiences a downturn. However, when the signature social program is providing economic value that covers at least a portion of its cost, the pressure to reduce support will be less. Asking for money each year is painful and unreliable whether the program is internal or external. It really helps to start with a known commitment from a firm.

Second, it improves access to a firm's resources. When a signature social program is integrated into a firm's culture, business strategy, and operations, the firm's organization gains understanding and acceptance within the firm. This means that opportunities to use the firm's assets, including people and expertise, to the benefit of the signature program are more visible and accessible. The connection will increase the likelihood that influential people in the firm will know about and support the signature programs. A communication budget of a business will usually be huge in comparison to that of any signature social program. If that budget can be accessed, perhaps with a regular branded fund-raising event, a game-changing level of signature program visibility and engagement becomes possible.

Third, the signature social program receives an endorsement from an established firm or business that provides credibility. Most stakeholders are not going to analyze the quality of a signature program. However, an endorsing business will do just that. The firm's endorsement means that they have done research and concluded that the signature program is addressing a real need effectively and efficiently. That type of credibility is not easily obtained in any other way.

The Internal Signature Program

When the signature social program is an internal one, such as Dove Self-Esteem, or Salesforce's Philanthropy Cloud, the challenge of the signature program team is to actively manage the relationship with the sponsoring firm so that the program's purpose and approach are understood and the passion from helping real people in need is shared. The program should not be an appendage but part of the firm's values and culture.

To address this challenge, a communication channel and professional relationship between the people in the business, particularly the marketing staff, and those in the signature social program is needed. The business marketing team should believe that the signature social program should be integrated into their efforts to manage the visibility, image, and loyalty of the business brand. In most cases, signature programs will potentially be able to add energy, liking, and appreciation for societal values to the image of a business brand.

Becoming a Team

The integration should result in a **teamwork context**. A signature program or possibly a group of them, will become part of a larger team that includes a firm or business. Working as a team with organizational units and their people can be game-changing. It can result in access to insight and talent that would otherwise be missing and in processes that can lead to a signature program with a more coherent strategy and more capable tactical efforts. Further, a team with the right people, committed leaders, and a clarity of mission can lift morale as well as improve performance.

The more traditional method is to have silos, a business silo and a societal silo staffed by different types of people with different goals, guided by different values and culture, and having little or no association or communication. The resulting lack of contact and relationships inevitably means missing access to resources and performance enhancing opportunities. It also leads to competition for resources and a voice at the executive table. It is unhealthy but not inevitable.

How do you move from silos to teams? I did a study described in the book Spanning Silos based in part on interviews with over 40 CMOs who reported on their silo problems such as confused brands, missed opportunities, and misallocation of resources and on what worked to reduce these problems.[76] The core conclusion—do anything that replaces isolation and competition between silos with communication and cooperation.

Some ways that a signature social program can encourage communication and cooperation and a team atmosphere are to:

- Get appropriate people from the sponsoring firm or business to be involved in the creation or the review of the purpose/mission, vision, and goals.
- Have an employee volunteer program.
- Have involving fundraising programs.
- Encourage the collaboration with people on the business side, especially specialists and those in the marketing arena.
- Create an advisory council with people in the business silo perhaps including people with helpful backgrounds or knowledge outside the firm.
- Create task forces with people in the business silo that could be charged with specific tasks such as reviewing the signature social brand vision or suggesting refinements or augmentation to the service being provided.
- Sponsor podcasts, hold events, or publish a newsletter that involves and attracts people in the sponsoring firm or business.

The Nonprofit External Signature Program

A nonprofit should strive to find firms that will adopt it as one of the firm's signature social programs. The right firm will commit to an active, long-term partnership relationship that will go beyond donating or cause marketing (where a portion of the sales price of their product goes to the nonprofit) or grants of money. The nonprofit team will then manage the link between the two brands. A fit will have to be recognized or created. In either case, the motivation needs to d to be based on passion for the societal need and not simply to gain favorable publicity. Although the initiative for the union now comes from the nonprofit and its program rather than the business. the driving forces, the criteria, and the goals will be similar.

An external nonprofit gets the three benefits noted above, a stable source of funding over time, access to a firm's knowledge and resources, and the credibility that comes from an endorsement. The firm who adopts the nonprofit gets a tested program over an established need area that already has a brand. There is no need to create a start-up with significant investment and risk. It is a win-win. The path to this outcome is available but underused partially because nonprofits are not aggressive in seeking it out but also because there is inadequate search and creative thinking among firms.

One problem is that nonprofits, familiar and comfortable with conventional fund raising, are not used to seeking out long-term partners, developing a brand mindset that would make that effort effective, and, in general, using branding methods. It will often take a new perspective and set of skills. It is not easy of course, but the payoff is significant.

Targeting. To get business partners a plan is needed. The search starts by identifying prospective partners. One set could come from firms or people within firms that are currently contributing by donating, volunteering, or providing resources. Can their participation be explicitly valued, recognized, and gently elevated? Perhaps they would be candidates for a board seat or an advisory group.

To expand that set, consider what specific would fit best with the purpose or mission and operation of your nonprofit. How would the integration work? What exactly would your nonprofit do to their brand with respect to employees and their external stakeholders? Then comes patience. Bringing them up the involvement ladder may take time, a strategy, the nurturing of contacts, and people to make it happen.

Building relationships. It is about relationship building. Relationship are not a one-way street. It cannot be only what is great about your program and what they can do to help. It is also about them, their strategies, and goals. What are their needs and interests? How can the structure of Chapter 8 be used to frame the conversation? Relationship are between people but also between organizations. Getting a business organization to become involved in some way perhaps by providing volunteers is a beginning to a relationship.

Many nonprofits such as Habitat for Humanity have tiers of sponsorship. So it can be relatively easy for a firm to jump on a lower rung of the ladder. They are then involved and the task is to move them up the ladder. An analysis of what an integration would look like between the organizations and how that could be implemented might help especially if there were inputs from both teams.

Priorities. Then there is a need to establish priorities. How many relationships can be pursued at the highest level? At the next level? For the most attractive businesses, there should be a strategy that could require years of investment and planned interactions using multiple connections. The priority list can be dynamic as connections emerge, grow, or recede.

Linking the Signature Program to the Business

The nature and strength with which the program is linked to the business brand is critical. A great program, if not linked, is not receiving an endorsement nor providing value to a business. The need is to connect without compromising authenticity. The more it is linked visually, logically, strategically, and organizationally, the more likely the values and reputation of the signature social brand will benefit from the endorsement and therefore enhance the business.

We now turn to Part IV, on building a strong brand for the signature social program. The methods will apply to an umbrella social program as well.

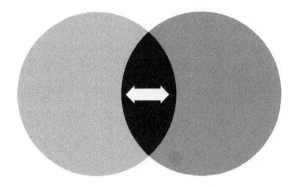

Part IV

PUTTING SIGNATURE SOCIAL BRANDS ON STEROIDS—FIVE BRANDING "MUST DOS"

Part IV puts us in the shoes of the social program leadership. How can they address the imperative to build a vigorous strong signature social brand, a brand that can help in accomplishing its two jobs—impacting a societal need and enhancing a business brand?

Chapter 10 discusses the importance of engaging all forms of established brand building methods and highlights several.

In Chapters 11 through 15, five branding "must dos" are described. Each has the potential to enhance the signature social brand. Collectively, they can put it on "on steroids." These five were selected because of their potential power and because they are underused and even under the radar to some firms.

- Chapter 11 Must Do 1—Create a North Star Direction to Guide and Inspire

- Chapter 12 Must Do 2—Find and Employ Signature Stories
- Chapter 13 Must Do 3—Create Brand Communities
- Chapter 14 Must Do 4—Identify & Fire "Silver Bullet" Brands
- Chapter 15 Must Do 5—Scale the Signature Program and its Brand.

Chapter 10

BUILDING INSPIRING SIGNATURE SOCIAL BRANDS

Tell me and I will forget, teach me and I will remember,
involve me and I will learn.
Attributed to Benjamin Franklin

For the signature social program to perform at impacting a societal need or enhancing a business brand, it needs a strong brand, a brand with energy, meaning, and emotional appeal. One brand-building route, described in the last chapter, is to have an active business partner that offers an endorsement and access to resources. The other, which is the subject of Part IV of the book, is to engage in all forms of brand building to build the signature social brand. Several suggested brand building concepts and tools are introduced in this chapter including five that are labeled branding "must dos" and are described more fully in five subsequent chapters.

Branding is crucial to making a program thrive. Just knowing that the program was branded signals a long-term commitment by the signature social program and its sponsoring business. It also provides the basis for how the brand is perceived, why it should be respected and even admired, and how it can engage and even foster passion.

A brand makes communicating the signature program more efficient, feasible, and memorable because it is a vehicle that summarizes a large volume of information. A new communication can remind, reinforce, or augment the understanding of a brand for which a base knowledge has been established. It does not have to communicate the details to an audience unmotivated to process new or complex information. The ingredients of Aunt Mabel's special soup are not needed, it is just the overall expectation of the experience that is summarized in its "brand."

The creation and activation of a strong brand can draw upon a host of proven brand building tools across campaigns, events, experiences, content, and voice. Consider some case studies already presented:

- Dove—The program and its communication involved a topic of personal interest to the audience—Real Beauty and Self-Esteem for teens—with novel experiments.
- Ben & Jerry's—Flamboyant stunts and forceful, timely positions on issues attracted attention.
- Salesforce—integrated the signature program story with the business offerings and leveraged the legacy founder story and the 1-1-1 program.
- Prophet—used subbrands to tie employee influenced signature programs together.
- Goldman Sachs—had comprehensive credible programs with intriguing, descriptive brands.
- Walmart—tied a comprehensive set of environmental programs to perhaps the most visible society need.
- Barclays—used stories to breakthrough.
- Habitat for Humanity—as noted in the last chapter, was a credible concept competently executed and leveraged with 90 plus business partners.

Some suggestions to consider: brand building strategy fundamentals, brand building vehicle options, and five branding "Must Dos."

Brand Building Strategy Fundamentals

Know your audience. The various stakeholders including employees, volunteers, donors, and sponsoring firms will have different perspectives, objectives, and exposure to different media vehicles. A tradeoff will need to be made. One approach is to have a message that efficiently reaches everyone, although the message might be interpreted differently by the various audiences. Another approach is to use multiple messages, each tailored to a specific stakeholder group or subgroup. A third provides a common general message supplemented with a more directed one. However, you should always put yourself in the shoes of the audience member, instead of focusing on what you want them to know. What will attract and interest?

Internal branding. Employees of the sponsoring firm as well as those of the signature social program crave meaning in their professional life and are often an important target. Communicating the program internally, to get employees to buy-in, and even to become actively involved in the signature program, becomes critical. It might be worthwhile to nominate a firm executive to be the champion of the signature social brand or one of its pillars with the responsibility of ensuring that a brand building effort is being implemented.

Instill visibility and energy. Visibility within a stakeholder group is necessary for the signature program to be relevant in any context for any purpose. A program that is unknown, is simply not there. Any brand also needs energy. It not only creates visibility but also, amazingly, can symbolize success, innovation, commitment, substance, and acceptance. It can come from many sources including new offerings, brand building events, thought leadership or an emotional connection. Recall the three Lifebuoy videos that touched people emotionally by recounting the application of the "Help a Child Reach 5" program through the eyes of a mother. They got 44 million views. That is visibility and energy. Also recall the irreverent stunts that Salesforce conducted such as the mock protest of "obsolete software" which attracted press attention to the "feisty pathbreaking newcomer."

Be credible and look for proof points. The task is really to get people to understand the logic of the signature program and why it is making a difference. Credibility can be enhanced by vivid impact stories, market tests, before-after experiments or just reporting results. Sometimes the detailing of inputs, the amount of grant money, the extent of volunteer time, or the number of people reached by the program can help. To counter the skeptical who compare the program size with the size of the firm or business, report a percent of sales or employees working time.

Brand loyalty. A brand goal is to create a connection with the signature social program's stakeholders that comes from trust, affinity, shared interests, pride and even inspiration. There should be a buy-in and a "I believe" attachment to the signature programs. There should also be an effort to gain engagement. For employees, that can mean volunteering. For others, an annual fund-raising event can provide engagement as well as energy and visibility.

Brand Building Vehicle Option

Leverage the website. The social program website is a key communication and engagement tool. It is important to get it right and to improve and augment it over time to reflect learnings and to send a signal that innovation and results are high priorities. Some questions. What are the needs and goals of each of the stakeholder audiences? What content will provide practical information, as well as energy, entertainment, and brand enhancement to visitors? Will it support brand building programs? Is the website functionally easy to use, not frustrating, and visually pleasing?

Social media. This is where much of the audience is and where there is a potential to get (free) pass along message exposure, with the home run being a story that goes viral. Success means the right staffing, content, and timing. Not easy.

New and innovative brand building. Be creative, look at what would draw people in. consider home run brand-building programs achieved for other brands in other industries and adapt them to your context. This could involve novel events, stunts, or fundraisers.

An NFT (nonfungible tokens) is an example of how a new technology can provide a fresh take on brand building. An NFT is an ownable, unique symbol which could be variant of part of a visual or video that is connected to the signature social program. It is similar to owning an original painting—there may be thousands of copies but only one original.

An NFT around a symbol of the signature social brand might be a way to elevate the loyalty of some to the signature brand. More likely, a sponsoring firm could have a NFT based promotion with the proceeds going to a signature social program. A NFT has been used to commemorate or promote a symbol (RayBan glasses), a core category pillar (Nivea paintings about the power of touch), an event (Gucci introducing a new line), or an offering (Taco Bell signature items). In most cases, the NFT efforts allocate the proceeds to a nonprofit. The challenge is to be creative about finding a fit with the signature social program.

Fund raising events have the potential to be a key brand builder for nonprofits, especially if they are regular events over many years and can engage people. A common mistake is to believe that fund raising events are mainly to raise money and to get receptive people to pull the donation trigger. There are other goals that usually are more important—namely to create visibility, energy, and engagement for the signature program for all the stakeholders including employees, donors, suppliers, and program participants. It is a place to deliver self-expressive benefits—"I am part of this, it represents what I do." When budgeting and planning the event, you should be more concerned with whether a feature will improve the interest and experience and be less concerned with whether its cost will decrease the net proceeds.

Of particular importance is the relationship between a fund-raising event and the creation and nurturing of a sponsor relationship. It can be a way to get a foot-in-the-door. A potential sponsor starts with having a table or two, with those attending becoming informed, impressed, and engaged. They, in turn, can become in-firm supporters of the nonprofit. That can lead to becoming advisors or being on the board. At that time, it will be more comfortable proposing that the firm become a major active sponsor, with the nonprofit being one of its signature social programs. It can start with proposing one table at one fundraiser.

Becoming a thought leader. Credibility, stature, and learning come from being a thought leader, which can be demonstrated with podcasts, articles, hosting meetings of experts, discussing issues on media outlets, researching problems and issues, and innovating by always trying new features and programs, being out in front. Patagonia, described in Chapter 11, is a thought leader as evidenced by programs to use organic or recycled materials, leadership in industry action, and ongoing advocacy.

Creating a visual representation of the brand which can involve the color and font of the brand name, logo, and tagline in various contexts. In general, the role of graphics on the website and elsewhere can make a difference in communicating the personality of the signature brand. When the visuals are consistent with the strategic message, communication will go better.

Brand Building "Must Dos"

The remining five brand building concepts and tools, shown in Figure 9-1, are termed "must dos" because they potentially will put the signature social brand on "steroids" and because they are often not considered or underleveraged. Each is elaborated in one of the next five chapters and are shown in Figure 9-1.

Figure 10-1

FIVE BRANDING "MUST DOS"

Create a brand North Star. The program needs guidance and inspiration based on a brand purpose or mission, vision, position, and tagline.

Create brand communities. A powerful way to connect is to foster brand communities, groups of people that share interests, activities, problems, or opinions, with the brand being an active member of the group.

Use stories. The way to combat disinterest and counterarguing, is to find or create "signature" stories that have a WOW factor with an exceptional ability to entertain, inform, intrigue, or involve.

Develop and use silver bullet brands. These are branded features, services, a founder, a story, an endorser or other "secret sources" that provides energy, differentiation, or credibility.

Scale the program. If the program is successful, its impact can be multiplied many fold by replicated it to other geographies or target audiences.

The next five chapters, Chapters 10 to 14, describe these five branding "must dos."

- Chapter 11 Must Do 1—Create a North Star Direction to Clarify, Guide and Inspire .
- Chapter 12 Must Do 2—Activate Brand Communities.
- Chapter 13 Must Do 3—Find and Employ Signature Stories.
- Chapter 14 Must Do 4—Identify and Fire "Silver Bullet" brands.
- Chapter 15 Must Do 5—Scale your Signature Social Program.

Chapter 11

MUST-DO 1
CREATE A NORTH STAR
DIRECTION TO CLARIFY,
GUIDE & INSPIRE

Vision without action is a daydream.
Action without a mission is a nightmare.
Japanese proverb

White Pony Express—Love in Action

It was the summer of 2013 when Dr. Carol Weyland Conner, so troubled by the thousands of people that go hungry while grocers, retailers, food manufacturers and restaurants often are discarding thousands of pounds of high-quality fresh food everyday due to artificially created "sell by" dates, excess inventory, or simply because it doesn't meet presentation standards, decided to start a food rescue program. Branded the White Pony Express (WPE), surplus food would be identified and delivered to organizations that serve those in need. Shortly thereafter, the White Pony General Store Program was added to rescue clothing and other items, such as toys and books, targeted for waste disposal because they were no longer being used or because of a cosmetic imperfection. These items were also to be shared with those that needed a boost.

The WPE mission is to "eliminate hunger and poverty by delivering the abundance all around us to those in need–with love." The mission guides and inspires WPE and its brand and is supported by five pillars that differentiate and energize.

Love in action. "With love" is not an afterthought. White Pony Express is serious about harnessing the power of love. It is part of its rationale, vocabulary, culture and actions. Volunteers, donors, partners, and recipients feel it. It starts with its heritage. The founder, Dr. Conner has made many observations about love and its role in WPE including—*"An act of helpfulness, a word of comfort, the spontaneous warmth of selfless love, gives to others what they greatly need. Their natural thoughts of gratitude and goodwill that flow from this, the heightened surge of their spirit, and the increased flow of pure love released by a selfless act bring to the giver infinitely more than he or she can ever give. Then at last is unlocked the key to lasting happiness!"*

White Pony Express is not about generous donors giving to needy recipients but, rather from an inner consciousness that makes it natural for all to help one another. It is about an uplifting Circle of Giving that starts with a donor offering food or clothing, a "runner" picking it up and delivering it to a recipient organization that passes it on to those that need help. The people in need gain functional assistance but also a feeling that someone cares and acted to make a difference. This feeling experienced by recipients then permeates the circle affecting all the participants. When the circle repeats, the shared feeling grows. As the WPE tagline says—"all of us taking care of all of us."

More than food. Unlike food banks WPE serves the need with more than food. It provides clothing which can be just as needed. In addition, there are other items, such as toys and books, that go beyond survival to bring joy, especially to youngsters.

Rescuing needed food and clothing etc. WPE emphasizes a rescue strategy. WPE enables those who are blessed with more than they can use to easily give to those in need, so that all can share in the abundance of life. WPE acts as a connecter. These items would otherwise be directed to a waste repository, sometimes with non-trivial expense and inconvenience, a tragedy given the needs of many.

Personalized. The food and clothing are tailored to the needs of the recipient and sometimes their needs are not clear without some inquiry. The "gifts" are not handouts but one that you would give your family or friends. The clothing, toys etc. are sometimes wrapped with a bow and folded just right to make it feel special.

Operating competence. Connecting those with abundance with those in need is a job that WPE does with amazing speed and reliability. WPE generally provides same day or next day delivery of items picked up with the reliability and passion reminiscent of its namesake, the Pony Express that revolutionized the old West over a century ago. The process, layered with respect and love, is built with partners and friends—volunteers, donors, food rescue product partners, general store product partners and recipient organizations—that have bought into the spirit of all of us taking care of all of us. It takes a village for sure.

When a brand and its culture is supported by both a head (logical) and heart (emotional), it will be stronger and have a more committed set of stakeholders. WPE with their concept of rescuing food and clothing etc. and their shear ability to get those items to people in need fast and reliably, scores high on the "head analysis" and the intensity and consistency of the "heart side" elevates all that they do and the people that do it.

In 2021, White Pony Express celebrated the major milestone of 17 million pounds of food rescued and delivered, and over 700,000 items of clothing, books, and shoes distributed since the founding. They were also making strides toward helping others create similar organizations.

After the societal challenge is identified and a signature social program has been conceived, the next strategic task is to create a brand for the program. It should be a signature social brand that is strong. Such a brand will be a principle driver of moving toward the integration of the signature program and the business strategy. It is a vehicle to guide the program to success in impacting a societal need, communicate that success, and create energy and an attractive image that will enhance a business and motivate it to become an active partner. All tasks that are necessary for the integration to emerge.

This chapter, the first of the five branding "must dos,' starts the brand-building process with developing an aspirational, but doable, North Star direction. The challenge is to create a brand that inspires, feels authentic, is credible and provides guidance to employees and the other stakeholders that interact with or have a meaningful connection to the signature program. That involves sets of questions. Why should all stakeholders, but particularly staff and volunteers, be proud of the program and their role? What is the compelling societal challenge that is addressed? How does the signature program address it effectively? What will be the program's impact? How can it be communicated internally and externally?

There are several conceptual tools that provide vehicles to address these questions. Each communicates in a way that guides and inspires. We focus on four of them. Each is presented with an alternative label because it is useful to consolidate concepts by connecting a pair of labels that are very similar, if not identical, in meaning and function. Each can be elaborated.

1. **Purpose (or mission)** statement that provides a compact expression of the essence of the program.
2. **Brand vision (or brand identity)** which creates pillars (or principles) that will serve to deliver credibility, points of differentiation and inspiration.
3. **Brand positioning (or framing)** that reflects what elements of the brand vision will be communication priorities to the various stakeholders.
4. **Tagline (or slogan)** that intrigues, inspires, informs, and anchors the external communication.

There are, therefore, a team of constructs. The purpose or mission does not have to do it by itself and should not be evaluated in isolation. Further, there are other constructs that are available for use as well. Among them are promises or value propositions (compelling benefit or experiences offered by the program), goals or aspirations (how many will be touched by the program and in what way) and organizational values (the core principles to manage by).

Purpose or Mission

The North Star for a signature social program or brand starts with its purpose or mission, concepts introduced in chapter 1 and used in chapter 5 in the text of a business or firm. Here we are in the shoes of the leaders of a signature social program.

A purpose or mission is usually a single sentence or phrase. The goal is to represent the essence of the signature program in a way that is perceived by employees, volunteers, sponsoring businesses, and other stakeholders as inspirational, authentic, credible, and capable of providing strategic guidance on the scope and approach of the signature social program. It should also be intriguing, be differentiated from other programs. The purpose/mission task is challenging but it should be clear that its primary role is usually to remind and reinforce rather than to reach those that are unfamiliar with the brand.

Some role models.

- Goldman's 10,000 Women program—*"to help grow local economies and bring about greater shared prosperity and social change by providing 10,000 underserved women with a business and management education."* Puts a Goldman competence aura over a social good goal.
- Lifebuoy's "Help a Child Reach 5"—*"to save lives by spreading he importance of good handwashing habits around the world."* Saving lives around the world is ambitious and inspiring.
- Doctors without Borders—*"provides impartial medical relief to the victims of war, disease, and natural or man-made disaster, without regard to race, religion, or political affiliation."* It makes the point that its organization, unlike others with a similar mission, is there to serve anyone, with no restrictions and no qualifications.
- Oakland Promise—*"is engaging the Oakland community to advance equity and economic mobility through cradle to college and career achievement."* Its clear and unique "cradle to career" scope sets it apart from other groups addressing upward mobility barriers.
- One Tree Planted—*"to reforest the planet one tree at a time. $1 donated helps plant one tree, it's that simple."* It is that simple.

- charity: water—*"help bring clean and safe water to every person on the planet"* involves an ambitious goal that in context of its accomplishments seems aspirational reflecting passion rather than empty promises or grandiose wishful thinking.

It can be helpful to elaborate on the purpose or mission to provide more depth, breath, and clarity. The elaboration can take the form of visuals, stories, or descriptions of the societal need or signature program. Some examples:

- Dove self-esteem program wants to *"ensure that the next generation grows up enjoying a positive relationship with the way they look—helping young people raise their self-esteem and realize their full potential."* To this is added "We've partnered with leading experts in the fields of psychology, health, and body image to create a program of evidence-based resources, including parenting advice, to help young people form healthy friendships, overcome body image issues, and be their best selves." This elaboration provides the substance that is needed to provide credibility as well as inspiration

- Teach For America "finds, develops, and supports a diverse network of leaders, working together to end educational inequity." The elaboration—"the program connects, gains depth and adds passion, when its eight values are added—a commitment to pursue equity, strengthen community, achieve impact, choose courage, act with humility, demonstrate resilience, learn continuously, and strive for diversity and inclusiveness."[77] The use of values provides substance and texture.

- The American Red Cross *"prevents and alleviates human suffering in the face of emergencies by mobilizing the power of volunteers and the generosity of donors"* adds stories to give the strong statement an emotional anchor.

- The Make A Wish foundation—*"Together, we create life-changing wishes for children with critical illnesses"*—just needs to add a picture or video of a child saying "I wish...."

Note that in all these cases the purpose or mission, even those with stretch goals, has authenticity and credibility. It is what the organization does and is fueled with passion, heritage, and resources.

Creating a purpose or mission that has authenticity and credibility, while also being able to guide, enable, and inspire is not easy. It takes work to have something that really clicks for multiple stakeholders. A purpose or mission can be too shallow or bland to be inspiring or even to have meaningful content. It can also be so specific that it prevents rather than enables entrepreneurial thinking in the societal impact sphere. Sometimes it can take a long time and several iterations to get it right.

Brand Vision (or Brand Identity)

A signature social program needs a brand vision (or brand identity) to inspire and guide.

A brand vision is the aspirational, multidimensional set of **"pillars" (or "principles")** of what the brand should stand for in the eyes of clients, employees, and other stakeholders. In a building, a pillar is a column that supports a heavy component, like a roof. In branding, a pillar supports the brand's vision with substance and relevance. It answers questions like: What should come to mind when the brand is encountered? What are the perceptions and opinions? What are the bases of a brand relationship? What aspects of the brand will drive the business strategy and relationships with customers, employees, and other stakeholders?

The brand vision is aspirational and can differ from a current brand image. It is the associations the brand needs to have going forward, given its current and future strategy. In some contexts, a brand needs to improve on some characteristics in order to remedy a weakness or to enhance or extend its mission. However, the brand vision also needs credibility. There must be proof points showing that an aspirational pillar will happen based upon programs in place or planned. It cannot be simply a wish.

The brand pillars are not built from a prespecified check list, a "one size fits all, fill in the box" model that may contain irrelevant items. Nor are pillars excluded because they lack a "box." Pillars are created that are relevant for the context at hand and could be defined in a variety of ways—a program attribute, organizational values or culture, nature of the societal need, a technology, or process used. It is your brand and your context. Whatever works for you should be included.

The brand vision is nearly always multidimensional because social programs (with few exceptions) cannot be defined by a single thought or phrase. There could be as many as 10 to 12 brand pillars. A few that are the most compelling and differentiating are selected to be "core brand pillars" which will be the primary drivers of brand-building programs and initiatives. They will be on the front lines to clarify, inspire, and guide.

The remaining brand pillars, termed extended brand pillars, provide texture and breadth to the brand vision, a home for brand aspects of the brand that may not merit being in the core perhaps because they are not a basis for differentiation. An extended brand pillar sometimes gets elevated as the process reevaluates. That happened to BerkeleyHaas, where "confidence without attitude," was a member of the extended brand vision but turned out to be the most differentiating and compelling core pillar after it earned its promotion.

Figure 10-1 provides an example of how a brand vison might be structured and filled out.

Figure 10-1

A POSSIBLE BRAND VISON FOR "HELP A CHILD REACH 5"

Core Brand Pillars

Real Kids and Real Parents
- Two million kids die before they reach 5 each year
- Utari, a mom of one of the unlucky boys, remembered his birthday

Handwashing Saves Lives
- Thesgora Village programs reduced diarrhea from 36% to 6%
- "Help a Child Reach 5" programs reduce diarrhea by 45% and pneumonia by 23% worldwide

Not Just Handwashing But the Right Handwashing
- How: 20 seconds five occasions during the day
- Photo device that illuminates germs after a hand wash illustrates

School Programs that Involve and Work
- Five superheroes
- Volunteers: Employees and youth initiatives

Goal
- A billion people washing hands properly

Extended Brand Pillars

Global Handwashing Day
- Lifebuoy is a founding partner
- Over 500 million people in 100 countries join to celebrate handwashing

Lifebuoy Health Heritage
- 1889 William Lever introduces lifebuoy Soap to make hygiene accessible to all
- Combat Cholera in Victorian England

Unilever Compass (Successor to the USLP)
- Protecting the planet: CO2 attack, waste reduction, water usage
- Improving health and self-confidence

What characterizes a brand pillar? What is needed to enable the vision to do its job of clarifying, inspiring, and guiding? There is a set of criteria, a wish list. Each pillar does not need to have all of them. However, collectively the brand vision should exhibit these qualities. It should:

- **Resonate with stakeholders**. There should be parts that sing—this works for me. It is relevant to what I do and what I want. The vision should motivate and even inspire the organization's employees and partners. It should make them care. It should also instill pride, a feeling that "if we do this, it will make a difference."

- **Differentiate from other social programs**. There should be parts that are perceived as creative, clever, unique, and even newsworthy, making the brand vision ownable. It will be seen as the only brand with this vision profile.

- **Be credible**. This organization can pull this off. It has the credentials, resources, and commitment to make it happen.

- Stimulate action. A compelling brand vision will stimulate brand-building initiatives and programs and create energy to support action. It should also provide a guide as to priorities, which pillars need investment, and which should have a communication priority.

- **Overcome "reason-not-to-buy" barriers**. Addressing reasons not to participate in the program, such as "the overhead is too high," can be decisive in gaining relevance and success. This usually involves a parity goal, to be perceived as "good enough" on this dimension so that a perceived risk or inadequacy does not become a barrier.

There are some additional observations. First, the label for each pillar should be evocative, powerful, and memorable. The "real kids and real parents" label, for example, in the figure bring perceptions of actual people with stories. A label should at least have two words. It is important to beware of an understated claim that your brand is innovative, high quality or customer driven. This type of general claim, shared by many brands, needs to have your own different and credible take on it. If one pillar is leadership, for example, it should be leadership that is unique to the brand, such as Berkeley Leadership for the BerkeleyHaas school.

Second, the brand vision pillars should be elaborated with some bullet points or a few sentences that will add texture. Elaborations provide detail, proof points, facts, and relevant initiatives. When elaboration is missing, the labels will be subject to misinterpretation and distortion and may lack punch. In both the label and the elaboration, it is helpful to use branded features. The four superheroes and Global Handwashing Day are brands that serve to make the communication task much easier.

Third, there might be a need for multiple brand visions. A brand vision might need to be adjusted, by adding, deleting, changing the status, or reinterpreting a brand pillar for a particular stakeholder group, such as employees volunteers, or donors.

A well-executed brand vision makes a huge difference. It matters if the signature social program creates visibility and energy among its "customers" and other stakeholders. It matters if the program creates the right image, engenders respect if not awe, and is authentic or "on brand" in what it does and says. It matters if the "customer" and other stakeholders get committed to the organization and its goals. It really matters. A well-conceived brand and brand-building program can deliver. And its absence can result in losing enthusiasm or even acceptance of the signature program..

The brand vision is not set in concrete. It both represents and enables a program strategy. Therefore, if the program strategy changes, the brand vision must also change. The most effective brand vision pillars tend to have a long life. Consistency over media and time are the hallmarks of the strongest brands. However, in dynamic times changes occur and, in those cases, the brand vision needs to adapt to a new direction. It cannot be an hindrance or a reason not to go forward. As a result, it might be necessary to add, delete, or reinterpret vision pillars.

The process. The brand vision development process starts by asking the question—what should our brand stand for? What are our aspirational associations? These items, which often number between fifty and a hundred, are then grouped. Each group is given a label and becomes a brand pillar. This grouping and labeling process is crucial and difficult. It can take weeks and sometimes years to get the right grouping and right set of labels. The most impactful, in terms of resonating, differentiating, and having credibility, are assigned to the core pillar group.

It can be helpful to precede the process by putting a dozen or so signature stories on the table. That usually provides a broader perspective and the confidence for people that propose pillars that others think too ambitious. A story can provide evidence that a stretch idea is possible or even already within the capability of the organization.

The brand vision needs to be translated into effective communication. This requires a discussion of the concepts of positioning (or framing) and taglines (or slogans).

Positioning (or Framing)

The brand's position provides priorities to the communication programs. When the brand is mentioned or considered, what brand pillar or pillars should come to mind? Which will best differentiate, resonate and be deliverable? What perception will allow the brand to win acceptance and commitment?

What will be the brand position of "Help a Child Reach 5"? What should it include? What associations should take the lead? Is it a program that saves kid's lives, a program that affects real kids and real parents, or a program that involves an in-school program? Is it some combination of the above? The positioning strategy may change from audience to audience. It may be different for employees, donors, partner organizations, or for different client segments. The goal is to create a leadership position for the signature brand defined by a pillar or pillars that makes the brand most likely to achieve its goals of creating visibility, an enhanced image, and a stronger loyal following.

Framing. Positioning is about how the brand should be perceived. Framing is concerned with what dimensions are prominent in any discussion relevant to the brand and what dimensions are top-of-mind when making judgments or decisions in which the brand is involved. In each case, the goal is to prioritize one or more core pillars of the brand.

Framing the discussion can be critical because, in most cases, the quality of the persuasive argument is less influential than what the argument is about. Therefore, the right frame that includes the core brand pillars will stimulate the "right" conversation. However, if the frame omits these core pillars, the end result will be disappointing. White Pony Express differs from food banks, in part, because they deal with clothing and because the food and clothing they obtain is rescued. If WPE did not exist, much of that desperately needed product would have not only gone to waste but also absorbed costs and created environmental issues. WPE should, therefore, frame the discussion by ensuring that "clothing and rescue" are not ignored. That framing result may be more influential than arguing that their approach to rescuing clothing and food is superior.

Tagline (or Slogan)

A tagline is a phrase or sentence or two that represents and communicates the essence of the social program or organization behind it in a punchy, intriguing way. It should represent what you are and what you do in a way that that is memorable, perhaps by being humorous, emotionally touching, or visually eye catching. Think of the Good Hands People of Allstate with the visual of hands reaching out.

A tagline provides a flexible, often costless, way to communicate externally who you are and what you do. Wherever the brand and symbol appear, on trucks, websites, stationary, etc., there may be an option to include the tagline, often at no added cost. It can also remind and reinforce for internal audiences.

Sometimes the brand itself can be the tagline or be a complement to the tagline. Think of "Help a Child Reach 5," "Feeding America," "Pledge 1%," or "GreenWorks," or ." In each case, the name itself provides information about the essence of the program. It is a punchy, short statement of the purpose or mission and is itself a tagline.

In most cases, the name needs a separate tagline that will inform and intrigue. Consider the following taglines:

- Because the earth needs a good lawyer (EarthJustice)
- Clean Water. Healthy Fish. Happy People (Delaware River Watershed Initiative)
- Send a net. Save a life (Nothing but Nets)
- Would you care more if I was a panda (World-Wide Fund for Nature).
- All of us taking care of all of us (White Pony Express)

- ONE DOLLAR. ONE TREE. ONE PLANET. (One Tree Planted)

Notice how these short taglines can describe a purpose/mission, inspire, and provide emotional involvement in a compact and clever way. They are all catchy, clear, and memorable. Beware of a tagline that tries to do much or is too descriptive. It should instead reflect the most inspiring aspects of the brand vision and purpose/mission of the social program in a memorable way.

The **North Star** should guide and inspire, especially inside the organization. For employees, it should be an important motivation to show up and be a source of pride. It should have a key role in building and sustaining the culture and in determining what behavior and decisions fit the organization. Strong North Star statements will stand the test of time. However, as programs evolve and change, there should be a willingness to change or adapt the North Star guides to accommodate that change.

We now turn to the second branding "must do," brand communities.

Chapter 12

MUST-DO 2
CREATE BRAND COMMUNITIES

*"Every person is defined by the communities
he or she belongs to."*

Orson Scott Card, American author

Patagonia Has Heart

Patagonia has created several communities based on their passion, leadership, and heritage in the environmental space. The passion was there at the outset in 1972, when founder Yvon Chouinard helped to change rock climbing by introducing, Chocks, a replacement for metal pitons that were despoiling rock faces. It has expanded dramatically since with an inspirational mission formulated in 2018 to *"Save our home planet." Consider some background stories about Patagonia.*

One of Patagonia's brand pillars and major customer appeals is that its clothing and its operation are environmentally sensitive. Nearly 90% of its clothing material comes from recycled sources such as plastic containers, material scraps from the factory or discarded clothing, a practice that saves over 4 billion tons of CO_2 going into the atmosphere. The Nano Puff Jacket, for example, was changed in 2020 to use 100% postconsumer recycled polyester insulation which cut production emission by nearly a half.

In 2011, Patagonia ran an ad with the headline "Don't Buy This Jacket" in the New York Times on Black Friday, to encourage customers to break away from easily discarding garments that still work and, rather, buy only what they need. The ad, which features Patagonia's popular R2 Jacket, explains that 35 gallons (135 liters) of water and 20 pounds (9 kg) of CO2 went into its manufacture and much of that would be saved if customers could forgo a new one. It became a signature Patagonia ad and symbol. Think about it--customers are asked to not buy, in order to save our natural resources. Who does that?

A year later, Keith and Lauren Malloy created a blog around getting people to share stories about experiences involving their favorite Patagonia products and the rips, tears, patches, and stains that were reminders of special moments. As an aside, how many customers are that into any brand? Patagonia was inspired by the stories and decided to upgrade, expand, and energize their repair and recycling service. The result was Worn Wear, a signature program with a mission to extend the life of all the products that Patagonia makes. At Worn Wear, a person can return a Patagonia garment (for credit on a future purchase) to be recycled or repaired and resold. The program was supported with a large repair facility, a mobile repair service, and a full-scale used clothing business operated from a website.

In 1986, Patagonia began a policy of donating each year to environmental causes, an amount which became 1% of sales, calling it an "Earth tax." In 2002, it formed an organization called the "1% for the Planet" and asked other firms to join. By the year 2021, over 2,000 member companies in 45 countries said yes. The organization certifies that the 1% was actually spent by each member, and provides stories, some dramatic, that illustrate the action of the members. The member website contains the "One Planet Talks" section where pressing environmental issues are discussed in virtual events with leaders in the movement. The result was a Patagonia community of firms and their staff and followers that were coming together with a common sense of purpose and commitment.

Most Patagonia employees are activists as well. A few that have particular presence in a spot are selected to be Global Sport Activist and use their roles in a sport community to drive societal change.

Patagonia uses some of its 1% money to support local environmental nonprofits. This is a direction that started in the 1970s, when Patagonia adopted a group trying to protect the Ventura River, near Santa Barbara, CA from a development project that would affect salmon spawning and bird habitat. The effort succeeded and led to policies that reversed the river's decline. In addition to grants, every two years, Patagonia holds a Tools for Grassroots Actives Conference to teach marketing, campaign, and publicity skills to Patagonia linked nonprofits.

As a result of the 1% grant program screening, Patagonia created a list of organization doing effective work efficiently and in 2018 launched the Patagonia Action Works to connect customers and others to environmental action groups that Patagonia supports. Locally, Patagonia stores hold Action Works events to build a sense of community with the often underappreciated grassroots participants.

Patagonia helped gather the top leaders in the apparel industry, non-governmental organizations, academia, and the U.S. Environmental Protection Agency for an inaugural meeting in 2010 to determine the feasibility of working together to create an index of performance addressing societal problems. The result was the Sustainable Apparel Coalition which grew to over 50 firms representing nearly a third of all clothing and footwear sold on the planet.

More firm communities were formed as a result of additional initiatives. Patagonia has taken a leadership role in getting the private firms and local activists to push an environmental agenda. It started the We the Power campaign in Europe to get local forces to push for renewable electric production by non-traditional means, with an aim to create 45% of electricity by 2050. Patagonia has also founded or supported industry organizations that address governance issues regarding the working conditions and wages of those in offshore factories.

The net result—Patagonia is a leader or role model and umbrella brand for a broad Patagonia community and for a wide variety of more focused communities associated with signature social programs such as Worn Wear, 1% for the Planet.

The Sustainable Apparel Coalition, Patagonia Action Works, and dozens more. Some are subsets of Patagonia faithful and others are groups of firms and their stakeholders. Patagonia, by leveraging its voice and action via communities, is making a difference, and providing a place for people and firms to express their own values and mission. At Patagonia integration between business and social is not an issue because they are literally one.

Brand communities have enormous potential. A signature social program needs buy-in. However, a more ambitious goal, if possible, should be to gain involvement, commitment and even passion about the program. To do so involves the basics. It requires the development of a program that works operationally, does not disappoint, is run by competent people, and has an effective communication program to explain the why and how of the program. However, commitment and passion need more than the basics. This is where the idea of a brand community fits in.

A Brand Community

A brand community is a group of people or organizations with shared involvement or even passion in some activity, goal or interest area connected to a brand, a community that provides self-expressive benefits, a sense of belonging, usable information, social benefits, and engagement opportunities.

When all or part of a stakeholder group form a brand community, there is a different mindset on both sides. The organization and the brand team are no longer talking at the members and are no longer trying to convince or sell. They are part of the community and active teammates. The brand team and the community members are on the same side. That mindset changes everything, including perceptions, attitudes, reception to activities, and communication. It is not always possible to form or be a brand community, but it is worth trying. Even if there is a miss, getting there part way may be better than the alternative.

With each brand community, there will be a hierarchy of membership coded by their level of involvement and commitment. Some will be leaders and innovators, finding new issues, developing points of view, improving programs, or planning events. Others can involve active participation, by providing or consuming information, attending events, or engaging in social intercourse. Still others, who may not participate regularly, will benefit from knowing that there is a band of like-minded people that can be trusted and that accept you as a member. Consider Patagonia and the communities that it fosters.

Why a Community?

Why should a person not pursue an interest area on his or her own? What does a community provide? What is wrong with a firm that focuses on connecting with stakeholders by communicating the descriptions, goals, and benefit of its signature social programs without a community motivation?

I have been a Cal (U of Calif at Berkeley) Bears fan forever. It is very hard, because in basketball and football a rare outstanding year is near but never at the top, a good year is above average and neither happens with regularity. However, I spend time nearly every day keeping up with the news and rumors about players and coaches. During the season, on game day, I can be an emotional roller coaster ending with despair or ecstasy and end up discussing the results with a few similarly demented friends. It is really important to me that Cal wins or at least is respectable. I am a part of the Cal sports community. Although I have only a dozen or so fellow members that I communicate with regularly, I have a relationship with the others who I don't know but match my interest level and commitment. I belong. I share. I participate.

I am defined by my "membership" in not only the Cal community but also a group of authors called the Silicon Guide, the White Pony Express nonprofit, the Monument Crisis Center nonprofit, my high school class, and my extended family. I feel special when traveling because of the way I am recognized and treated by United Airlines and Hertz and am an advocate for both. These communities define who I am and provide meaning, support, and joy to my life.

Why should a community be so important? And how can a nonprofit create and nurture communities? One answer—a community provides value to its members in at least five ways—through self-expressive benefits, belonging, informational source, social benefits, tangible functional benefits. All five are in evidence in my own set of communities.

Self-Expressive Benefits

A brand community delivers self-expressive benefits, a way to express who you are. A part of finding meaning in relationships and life is communicating to yourself and others your identity. What is the true you? What do you believe? What are the important things in your life, the priorities? What adds meaning to the day-to-day activities?

It is not easy communicating the real you, especially the empathetic giving side because it can come off as self-serving and inflated, which is uncomfortable at best. Membership in a brand community around a signature social program, in contrast, can represent who you are with substance and without bragging. Being part of a brand community reflects:

How you spend your time and resources. What you do, how you spend your time and resources represents who you are. People hear what you say but are usually more impressed about what you do. A brand community representing a set of activities, goals or interests is a way to express your identity. By saying that a person is a member of H.O.G.'s (Harley Owners Group—the ultimate brand community), a supporter of the Avon Walk for Breast Cancer or Doctors without Borders, or a Salesforce volunteer in a school, makes a statement about his or her interests and activities.

Your values, what is important. A community that focuses on a societal issue will signal to others what is important in your life, a set of values that might be hard to communicate in another way because the community is tangibly credible. Think of the scary threat of climate change, the impact of breast cancer on family and friends, or the sight of small businesses failing. Having a societal problem such as these become a priority in your life and says a lot about the type of person you are.

Belonging

There is a feeling of belonging to a group where the brand is an active member. Belonging and being accepted is an important personal need, whether you are a fourth grader or an adult. The brand community provides a core circle of friends that are reliable, always there and always interested. People hunger for connection, and a brand community delivers. As involvement and commitment increase, of course, so does the sense of belonging. Being isolated, having to "do it myself" is the opposite of belonging and not very attractive.

AMEX created the Shop Small movement to help small businesses thrive when the economy was suffering. For shoppers, the movement communicated the feeling that comes from local shopping, plus the attraction of Shop Small promotions sponsored in part by AMEX. The result was a reframing of the retail space as charming and a community where they belonged. For retailers, AMEX offered a set of vented suppliers with AMEX negotiated discounts, payment authorization programs, help with posters and other visuals, and access to advice about all elements of managing a small business. Small retailers could now feel that they were no longer alone but part of a community with a solid coach.

Informational Benefits

The brand community will usually have a website that will answer questions, give suggestions, and provide information about community events, relevant books, and podcasts. Because the community focuses on an area of interest, it is likely to have information that is relevant to you. If two-way communication is possible, even though a chat room, it adds to its power to answer specific questions and address issues.

Trust in information from a brand community will be high. People from the community are interesting, often obsessed with the subject manner, and will not be superficial or create information from another source that might be suspected of being biased, phony or self-serving. Because a sponsoring brand is not in the context of being a seller but is now "one of us," the information from that source will be credible as well.

Even when active participation is unavailable, a brand community that provides a go-to place for current and relevant information can precipitate strong bonds. There can be an affinity without interaction. A good example is Gardena, the online garden tool firm, where there are over 500 in-depth tips on gardening organized by season that offer a valued go-to resource, despite being a place where most do not frequently interact. It provides useful information without bias from members of a meaningful reference group.

Social Benefits

A brand community delivers social benefits, by connecting to people that have similar values and interests. In some communities, you can have an active back and forth asking questions and giving opinions. Knowing that there is a group of like-minded people beside you provides social support. You are not alone in your views and interests. There are others who will respect and listen to you.

The power of social support has been shown in the social sciences. Having even one ally can be the support you need to defend a position that differed from the non-community group. Know that there is set of knowledgeable credible people sharing your interests and opinions can be comforting and empowering. The option of speaking out and having interactive conversations also addresses a basic need.

A brand community often comes with the potential to pursue social networking. The opportunity to network, making new connections and friends with industry peers, can result in more sources of ideas and commentaries and can lead to better job performance and even better jobs.

Tangible Functional Benefits

A member of the brand community should be made to feel special. One way to do this is to be recognized for past contributions and for being loyal. Events celebrating years of service and just being reminded that contributions are valued can help. The basic loyalty program idea of having tiers of loyalty (United as premier, gold, platinum 1K, for example) is a concept that can apply to societal programs. Just moving up the ladder can create a special feeling.

Feeling special can come from being an insider, being part of creating a strategy or improving operations. Small dinners or shared events, maybe at an off-site meeting, can tangibly demonstrate respect. Just showing that opinions are solicited and listened to can represent an indication that a person is valued.

Providing satisfying ways to engage can represent tangible benefits. The array of engagement options will be detailed next.

Engagement

All the rewards for a brand community—self-expression, belonging, informational benefits, social benefits, and tangible functional benefits will vary in intensity with the level of engagement. A healthy brand community will create engagement opportunities for its members, so that they will be more active and thus develop a deeper passion and commitment to its societal issues and programs. The goal is to move people from being passive members to increasingly higher levels of active, involved participation and, ultimately, to leadership roles.

It is important to note that even passive members can be a valuable part of the membership, even when their engagement is vicarious or remains in the potential category—"I might someday do this, there is that option." Their connection with the community does need to go beyond knowledge and acceptance to a belief that the community's interest and activities are worthwhile and match their own. Passive members that really care about and believe in the societal problems and issues can still receive self-expressive benefits and find comfort in the fact that others share their beliefs and concern. They are valuable, in part, because they might someday become active, because they will be recipients of the community information and can be conduits to others, and because they add a critical mass.

However, the challenge is to provide members with engagement opportunities that will reinforce and enhance their passion, commitment, and wiliness to share it with others. following are some ways to engage.

Become an Active Part of the Signature Program

Nearly all signature programs, internal or external, rely on volunteers. The volunteering options are endless, including "get your hands dirty" efforts. Brand community members could volunteer as discussion leaders for Dove's Self Esteem program. Firms could join Pledge 1% of Salesforce. Thrivent takes the pledge to another level.

Thrivent, a nonprofit financial services firm with a heritage of helping members of church communities, believes that humanity thrives when people make the most of all they've been given and that money is a tool not a goal. As a result, inspiring generosity and giving back is for it a core value. Each of the two million or so Thrivent clients and employees become part of a local Thrivent

Member Network, which was created in part to encourage and facilitate getting involved in helping others in need. It could be disaster relief, local projects, or building homes via Habitat for Humanity.

Any client or employee can propose a Thrivent Action Team to address a societal need with a specific program that could be a fundraiser, an educational event, or a service activity. The web site provides a roadmap to find, create, fund, and operate a program and a place to share the resulting experience and its impact with a story. Thrivent supports and the team brings the passion and will to make it happen. By 2022, there have been over 450,000 projects and over 50,000 stories of experiences emerging from the projects.

One major source of a team mission, initiated in 2005, is to participate building homes under Habitat for Humanity, which shares Thrivent values and goals. In the 16 years following the launch, Thrivent and its clients have contributed more than $275 million to help build, rehab or repair homes in the U.S. and across the globe. Thrivent employees and clients have also given more than 6.3 million volunteer hours to support Habitat's vision of a world where everyone has a decent place to live. Much of this effort is done under the Habitat and Thrivent "Faith Builds" branded program. The end product is no different from other Habitat homes but has a greater focus on volunteers from local Thrivent clients and Christian churches for volunteer and financial support.

There are several brand communities involved, the Thrivent Action Team that has organized a specific home building project, the larger Faith Builds community and the Thrivent member network community. All are functioning and can become relevant to an engaged individual.

An observation. Thrivent is an example of where a signature social program is fully integrated into the Thrivent culture and strategy and where the Habitat sponsorship delivers far more tangible benefits to Thrivent than it costs. It is not a question of allocating philanthropic grants to Habitant because it is a valued part of the Thrivent operating plan. It is also an example of the nonprofit that has almost no functional basis for a fit with this business partner. But they made it fit and made it work.

Participate in Money Raising Events

An example is the walk events used by the Susan G. Komen for the Cure, which was founded in 1984 by the sister of a cancer victim. In the early days of the organization, the "3-day" was created, a 60 mile walk for breast cancer as a major fund raising event. More recently, the More that Pink walk was introduced that provided a more flexible and accessible event for those that wanted to support the cause and celebrate those affected by breast cancer. Those participating become members of the ONE Community signifying the difference that one dollar, one story, and one step more can make in the fight. The community extends to friends, family, and supporters for the participants. They are all involved, in the training, event, and cause.

Interact with Community Members

Salesforce's Trailblazer community, for example, aspires to be pioneers, innovators, and lifelong learners, by employing the Salesforce array of products to find new ways to transform the experience they offer their own customers. Within the larger Trailblazer community, there are micro communities defined by product or application area. Some of these societal areas include sustainability, healthcare, education, philanthropy, and nonprofits. Members of these specialized units become a community and can try out ideas, ask for suggestions, raise an issue or problem, get comments, or just benefit from the ideas that flow from others, including some Salesforce experts.

Stimulate Discussion

There are several ways to create learning or stimulate discussion. One is to support the signature program by being a thought leader with sessions that explore the current problems and potential future directions that might lead to solutions. A global conference of solution researchers could be an option for some firms. Another is to be a learning vehicle to provide ways for community members to learn practical tools or learn about the history and nature of the social problem or issue on the table. A third is to be a library that brings together podcasts, articles, books etc. that are relevant to the societal issue.

Leadership Opportunities

A brand community's ultimate involvement is a leadership position—organizing events or activities and encouraging participation. Leaders can spread the word about the community, be external ambassadors, improve the operations, and participate in strategy discussions. If, for example, volunteer members take leadership roles creating and staffing courses relevant to a societal program, the number and accessibility is no longer limited by the program staff.

When Is a Brand Community a Brand Community?

How do you know that there is a brand community and not simply a description of an offering and its applications with a transactional relationship to its followers? There is no set of rules, but there is a degree of brand communityness that depends on how much the community delivers on the five dimensions of engagement. A strong score on two or more of the five would indicate that there is a functioning community that is worth supporting and nourishing.

Another is simply a mindset. If the brand and supporting organization believes that it is a community, and continuously supports and communicates it as such, then it is likely that a community exists or will emerge. Similarly, if the members believe that some of the five characters are there for them, a community will likely exist.

How Brand Communities Help Signature Brands

A brand community can be a significant asset to the signature social brand and its program by providing a set of committed people, many actively involved, as well as energy, visibility, and an enhanced positive image to the brand. Most notably, it is a asset different from others because its relationship to its members is unique, the most interested potential members are "taken," and it takes a significant investment to set up a community.

Committed stakeholders. The foremost value of a brand community is to provide a core, loyal stakeholder base, part of which is an advocate or ambassador spreading the news about the community and how it works.

Brand affinity. A person, in general, has a special affinity for others that share his or her passion, goals, and activities. If the brand is associated with that interest, it will also be regarded highly and if the brand is an actively involved partner and contributor, the bond will be greater. A person's' interest and passion will be channeled into the relevant communities and then to the associated brands.

Adds energy and visibility. All are critical elements of brand building that are difficult to achieve using conventional media and methods. Every time a person accesses the community, the brand is rewarded with some energy and visibility.

Ideas to improve or extend the program. The community can provide ideas and commentary on the signature program and the underlying societal challenges that can lead to a program enhancement or extension. This provides useful and timely information to the brand team and a feeling of being an active part of the community for the members.

Signature Programs Enable Brand Communities

Brand communities are powerful but not available to most business units. In most cases, their offerings are not capable of capturing the interest of a core customer base. Etsy, the craft site, offers a community of craft makers and buyers and the Salesforce Trailblazers community exists around involving software. However, there are the exceptions. Most offerings are not candidates to be the basis of a community because they and their offerings are not a focus of interest or an activity of importance to people or firms. Even when their offerings are connected to an activity, like tennis or hiking, there may already be communities and there is no need for another.

Signature social programs, in contrast, will usually be able to attract people who have or are capable of developing a deep interest in the motivating societal problems or issues and would benefit from and welcome a brand community. The net result, is that social communities will be a viable option for many signature programs.

Multiple Communities

A signature social program can have a set of communities that can stand alone or be a subset of a larger brand community. There can be "micro" communities for volunteers, doners and other supporters, partners and those that are involved in one of the signature program initiatives. They can all simultaneously belong to the "macro" committee that combines all of them into the larger group with more resources and a larger voice that becomes a vehicle for the "micro" communities to communicate and coordinate. The Thrivent story illustrates as does that of the White Pony Express and Salesforce Trailblazers.

The White Pony Express, the food and clothing bank described in Chapter 10, has a micro communities of operation volunteers, outside volunteers, and donors. They all have communication forums and regular meetings with stories, announcements, suggestions, and training. All participate in the macro community events and newsletters.

A business-based brand community can have a niche that is devoted to societal needs. Recall that the Salesforce Trailblazers is a community for all those that work with Salesforce offerings. There are Trailblazer subcommunities within each of the major categories. Some of these subcommunities, such as sustainability, nonprofits. philanthropy, and education are relevant to social problems and issues. Their presence in the larger community allows access to more resources and people with relevant experience and ideas.

Volunteers are especially likely to benefit from a community because they are organizational outsiders and are motivated by social benefits. A volunteer community can provide a structured way for volunteers to share problems and moments of joy or satisfaction with each other and to meet role models, who could provide ideas for improvement. The ability of volunteers to chat, comment, and suggest will increase the sense of engagement, social benefits, and commitment to the social program. These communities might even open up to volunteers from other organizations. The critical mass would be enlarged, as would the flow of social interchange and ideas. The interaction could result in partnerships or in a louder voice.

What Brand Community?

How can the right brand community that would support a game-changing market niche be found? Three questions can help.

- First, is there a **need** for a brand community? Will it attract a worthwhile group that will receive enough value add? Is there an opening for a new community or have others already gained a dominant presence? Recall

Patagonia who leveraged the passion for environmental issues to create a series of niches that attacked a viable group of firms or people. It was a matter of finding underserved needs and being creative.

- Second, can the **firm deliver** content, create a web site or organize meetings that will support the community? Can it be an active partner, by using its people or other assets?
- Third, can the community **get traction and be linked to the brand?** Will the proposed brand community programs get enough visibility, relevance, and credibility to be considered by target group members? Does it fit the brand?

Communities often find clue and inspiration from signature stories, which is the subject of Chapter 13.

Chapter 13

MUST-DO 3
FIND & EMPLOY SIGNATURE
STORIES

*We learn best—and change—from hearing
stories that strike a chord within us.*

John Kotter, Leadership Thought Leader

Early in the days of Prophet, the firm with which I have been associated, we volunteered at St. Anthony's during the holidays, an entity that provides a hot meal every day of the year in the inner city of San Francisco. During the first visit, a volunteer goes through a two- hour introduction that, in part, describes the program and provides many statistics, such as the percent of clients with dependency or mental health issues and the number of meals served.

They also told a story about a Palo Alto engineer who had to quit his job to care for his wife who had developed cancer. During the six-year caring experience, his insurance ran out, he had to sell his home and exhaust his savings. When she died he had no assets, his engineering talent had atrophied, and he was homeless and a client of St. Anthony's.

I soon forgot the descriptions and statistics, but I remembered the story and have shared it over 20 times in various forums. It makes a point vividly, albeit indirectly, in a way not possible with descriptions and statistics, that homelessness could happen to anyone. It is not restricted to addicts and the mentally ill.

Communicating a signature social brand and its impact to stakeholders is both difficult and critical. Signature stories can help address the challenge, in part because they have emotion and empathy in abundance. To see the power of stories, consider the following case studies.

The Natalia Story

Natalia was a 15-year-old girl in a small village in Mozambique. She had a life that revolved around water. Each morning, after caring for her six siblings, she would walk with pails to a riverbed and stand in line waiting to get dirty water from a hand-dug hole, a task that took hours. That meant she could go to school only twice each week. However, in 2012, thanks to charity: water, a nonprofit group that brings clean, safe drinking water to people in developing countries, her village received a well. This allowed residents to pump as much clean water as they needed, easily and quickly. Natalia was now always at school and on time. There were no exceptions.

The village's five-person water committee was tasked with developing and implementing a business plan to ensure the project's long-term sustainability and to educate the community about health, sanitation, and hygiene. When charity: water met with the committee, the last member stood to introduce herself—her feet wide apart, her arms crossed proudly, and with a pleased half-smile on her face: "My name is Natalia," she said. "I am the president." By far the youngest in such a position, Natalia was selected because of her confidence, tenacity, leadership skills and the fact that she could read and write. Her ambition has changed. She now plans to become a teacher and then a headmaster.

Her story captures the emotional relief and pride of accomplishment associated with a charity: water, whose nearly 23,000 projects in its first eight years have made clean water available to over seven million people.

The Cisco Stories

Cisco uses blogs and a website to communicate its societal programs using stories of Cisco employees or beneficiaries of signature social programs. The stories are real, you get to know the subject and what he or she accomplished. Here is a snapshot of two.

Cisco started Networking Academy in 1997, an education programs that empowers students to seek careers in IT, security, and networking, when it found that donating equipment was not working without people trained in their use. Over 23 million have been trained during their first quarter century. One individual was Ernest Wambari, who was attracted to a "genius wanted" sign at his college in Nairobi, Kenya in 2002. He tells how he expanded his technical and people skill sets, by working at several Cisco partner firms and getting a Cisco Certified Network Expert diploma. He ultimately landed a job in 2019 with the World Food Program. As an African, he felt that this role was meant for him.

Cisco developed the Cisco Tactical Operations (TacOps) team comprised of some 300 employee volunteers that are on call to build and maintain communication networks in disaster zones using satellite dishes and specialized software. Matthew Altman has been a TacOps engineer for 16 of his 22 years at Cisco. In 2010, after a massive 7.0-magnitude earthquake destroyed parts of Haiti, Matt worked within the rubble and participated in rescue efforts to get communications functioning in extreme working conditions. Seven years later, when a refugee crisis in northern Uganda reached its tipping point, he worked with partner and supplier firms to overcome some critical and difficult coordination issues.

KIND

KIND, a snack line founded by David Lubetzky in 2004, is the exemplar of healthy, natural, tasty snacks consisting of whole fruits and nuts, ingredients that "you can see and pronounce." Its name and purpose comes from three overlapping signature stories.

Lubetsky's father was suffering in a Nazi concentration camp, when, at considerable personal risk, a prison guard threw him a spoiled potato. This act of kindness meant a lot, both physically and emotionally, during a dark time.

When Lubetsky finished law school in 1993, inspired by the Oslo accords between the Palestinians and the Israelis, he started PeaceWorks an initiative to create economic cooperation between groups with a history of fighting each other. The theory was that if economic fortunes are tied, good feelings might replace hate. One venture was a firm that made sundried tomato paste, involving Israeli and Palestinian partners working together. The effort, albeit on a small scale, turned enemies into partners and colleagues.

In 2003, frustrated by the lack of healthy snacks, Lubetsky overcame manufacturing barriers to create KIND. It was called KIND because it is kind to your health and taste and because the firm was committed to fostering acts of kindness. It has #kindawesomeness cards, handed out to someone doing a kind act for someone else. The card has a website and code. A card recipient can check in and receive a package of KIND bars, along with another card for them to give to someone they spot doing an act of kindness. There have been 11 million documented acts of kindness as a result during the 15 years since its founding. Owning these acts of kindness provides a powerful brand connection and supports the purpose—"creating a kinder and healthier world - one act, one snack at a time."

HP My Story Storytelling Challenge

In partnership with the non-profit, Girl Rising, HP introduced "My storytelling challenge" in 2019. This allows young women around the world to share the personal stories that inspired them to launch local initiatives, some of which touched on difficult themes of racial injustice, sexual abuse, and child marriage. During its second year, the challenge drew 1,500 participants from 90 countries and created authentic, compelling stories. The impact went far beyond those participants because the concept touched people and some of the stories were widely exposed.

The stories expanded audience perspectives and gave confidence to the participants. Aryan from Afghanistan, age 15, told how she had trouble finding a lawyer for her refugee mom in Greece and vowed to become a lawyer. In her words, "being homeless was not in our hands. We were forced to leave our homeland and start a journey to Europe, the place where thousands of refugees are shouting for the meaning of freedom and humanity." Syahna, an 18-year-old San Diego high school senior, saw a plea on Facebook for purses to be donated to women at a homeless shelter. After a discussion with her father, she decided to try to find purses and add travel-sized toiletries. After persistent promotion on social media, the effort became a significant nonprofit called Purses for a Purpose, which collects donations and makes monthly visits to shelters with packed handbags.

Communication: The Role of Stories

A successful signature social program needs to communicate effectively to its program stakeholders in order to get their buy-in, involvement, and, hopefully, commitment to the program. Communication needs to go beyond understanding why the program is worthy. It needs to make visible the aspiration, empathy, and the emotion that prompted the program. It needs to reach hearts, as well as minds.

Often as important, is to communicate to employees and other stakeholders of a sponsoring firm or business. As noted in Chapter 8, societal investments that have little ability to enhance a business are likely to be misdirected, ineffective and have limited political support and internal momentum within the firm (or ongoing support from a corporate sponsor if a nonprofit). The ability of a signature program to help the business, such as improving employee commitment, increasing brand visibility, enhancing the brand image, and strengthening brand loyalty is dependent on creative and effective ways to communicate the signature program emotionally, as well as functionally, to the stakeholders.

The natural inclination when faced with this communication challenge, to put out program descriptions and accomplishments complete with compelling facts and logic, just does not work. People, in general, will not care about your program enough to even notice any communication. There is media clutter, information overload, competing and overlapping programs, and an "in-control" audience. The coping strategy of most people, when they hear about a new program or service idea, is to simply ignore it. Even if the communication is noticed and processed, the usual result is skepticism rather than persuasion and forgetting rather than changed perceptions and actions.

Enter stories. By stories we mean a "once about a time….." narrative that portrays actual or fictitious events or experiences. The core problem is that some people describe almost any kind of communication as a "story." A story as used here is not a set of bullet point facts or a description of a program, organization, or service. It is not a list of features or benefits. It may incorporate or motivate descriptions or facts, but in the context of a narrative.

Stories work when facts and descriptions do not. People perk up when they hear someone say, "Let me tell you a story." Just knowing that it is story sounds interesting. An arresting character or scene or a puzzling first sentence can draw you in. A really interesting story will prompt the golden goose of digital communication, a "share" to someone that will benefit by or be interested in the story because it is entertaining, fascinating or has useful information.

While descriptive material and facts are ignored, quickly forgotten, or greeted with skepticism, the same material, when embedded in or motivated by a story, will get through and will be processed. The empirical evidence from hundreds of studies dramatically shows that, in comparison to portrayals of descriptions or facts, stories are much better at getting attention, affecting perceptions, changing attitudes, being remembered, inspiring, and energizing.[78] They are not 20% or 30% better, but 200% to 300% better. The evidence is amazing. However, it only confirms what most know from personal experience and observation. Stories are what are noticed, enjoyed, remembered, and capable of changing or confirming opinions.

Signature Stories

This power does not reside with just any stories, **signature stories** are required. A signature story is a "once about a time…" narrative that is attention grabbing, involving, authentic, and containing (or motivating or illustrating) a strategic message. A signature story can be a strategic asset that provides visibility and energy to the signature social program and persuades or inspires employees and/or customers over an extended time. Consider its four characteristics.

First, it has a **WOW attention grabbing quality**, a "you have to hear (or see or read) this" reaction. It grabs attention because it is so intriguing, thought-provoking, novel, informative, inspiring, emotionally touching, exceptionally relevant, humorous or awe-creating. Without attention, nothing matters. Exposure to the story is not enough, because only small percentages of exposures are noticed and even fewer are processed. The story should be able to attract the eye and the mind. Think of a story that has stuck in your memory. It will almost surely be extremely high in one or more of these eight characteristics.

One measure of "WOW" is whether a story stimulates word-of-mouth communication personally and/or via social media. A case in point are the three Lifebuoy videos that describe the introduction of the "Help a Child Reach 5" program into three Indian villages that got 44 million views. They had "WOW."

Another measure is whether it sticks in your mind and gets remembered. That was illustrated by my San Francisco experience serving meals at St. Anthony's described in the beginning of the chapter. I have often remembered and shared the engineer story but soon forgot the facts to which I had been exposed.

Second, it is **involving**. The audience is drawn into the story, especially when there is detail that lets you visualize or feel the context. People empathize with the interesting characters and more so when they are vividly presented. The plot becomes a focus especially when it has a moment of tension, emotion, or humor.

The result is usually, but not always, a cognitive, emotional and/or behavioral response. Cognitively, the audience processes the story and its theme and accepts its major points. The challenge of walking for water each day is dramatized by Natalia's story. Emotionally, an involving story can precipitate feelings about the empathic characters and their role in the story. Pride in the charity: water program, and even more, in Natalia's ability to take on the chairman's job and create aspirational goals for herself can be overwhelming. Behaviorally, a story can motivate audience members to take action when the time is right. They might share the story or donate to charity: water and follow the progress of the well they supported.

Third, it has **authenticity**. This means that the audience does not perceive the story to be phony, contrived, or a transparent selling effort. Authenticity can come from the characters that feel real and are easy to empathize with. The story of Utari and the other "Help a Child Reach 5" mothers, for example, discussed in Chapter 10, provides the authenticity that comes from getting to know and admire a real person in a real setting. The storyteller, when perceived as objective and respected, can also contribute authenticity.

Authenticity requires substance behind the story and its strategic message in the form of transparency, policies, and programs. It cannot involve wishful thinking or puffery. Without supporting substance to confirm and solidify the strategic message, a story's authenticity is undercut and the brand is ultimately tarnished. Behind the Natalia story is charity: water, a program that provides a long-term source of water and does it at scale.

Fourth, a **strategic message** relevant to the audience needs to be contained in or supported by the story. A strategic message, as opposed to a tactical communication, will advance the essence of the signature social program. It will clarify or enhance, both internally and externally, some combination of its purpose/mission, the brand vision, the brand position, the aspirational customer relationship, the organization's culture, and the present and future business strategy.

The message can be embedded in the flow of the narrative. The Natalia story tells of the importance of the water council not explicitly but by how the council was chosen and its importance in the village. However, if there are still facts to be communicated that do not fit into the story, they can come before or after the story.

Place facts after to illustrate the story. In this option, the story gains the audience's attention, entices involvement into the context, distracts from counter-arguing, and provides a reason to process the facts that follow it. The story should provide a basis for believing the facts and for understanding that facts are needed to bring the story to completion and to show that it is more than an isolated anecdote. In the charity: water example, the story sets up the facts of the program—how many wells and how people are affected. The story makes these facts more relevant and interesting. The trick is to introduce the fact presentation so that it adds to or completes the story and does not diminish the story's authenticity by turning it into a selling experience or an exercise in puffery. If the story is compelling and well told, and if the fact presentation is relevant and compact, this risk is reduced.

Place facts before to motivate the story. The story's role is to illustrate what is behind facts such as the number of wells that charity: water has created with a glimpse of impact on a person and a village. The stories bring the facts to life with richness and vividness. There is a "let me illustrate what I am talking about" story moment. A facts-first strategy works when the facts themselves are punchy and at least somewhat intriguing—and are not drawn out. Felix Baumgartner went 24 miles up into the sky before jumping out. I want to hear more. Facts shouldn't make anyone lose interest before getting to the story.

A word of caution: The degree to which a signature story meets its four criteria—to be intriguing, involving, authentic, and with a strategic message—must be judged by those who develop and use it. However, they should resist the temptation to elevate to signature status a story that is weak in one or more of these four dimensions.

How a Signature Story Works

Signature stories work by making the strategic message get through. One reason is a story's ability to gain attention, critical in the era of media clutter, information overload, and competing messaging by others. Signature stories, by definition, gain attention. They also involve with a narrative that draws them in. However, there are five additional reasons why stories work. Stories:

Energize. A signature story and its content can provide energy to the signature social program as well as to the sponsoring business brand, especially a business brand that is surrounded by blandness and by offerings that are taken for granted. Just the fact that the signature story attracts attention can elevate. However, it may be so compelling that some people will share it. Energy is the secret sauce that helps any brand. It creates the perception of momentum, innovation, and the smell of success. Brands or programs that are stuck in the mud, not moving or advancing are often perceived as not the best choice, not relevant.

Distract from counter arguing, which is a primary reason that few change their minds, even when compelling facts are on the table. Audiences are skeptical of the facts and often the source or spokesperson. However, when the audience gets transported into the narrative that does not matter. You don't counterargue, it is just a story.

Recall the Barclays Digital Eagles case in Chapter 8, a volunteer force that taught people to thrive in the digital world. Stories around that effort were able to improve the Barclays trust score, that had been battered by their perceived role in the 2008 financial meltdown, and resisted conventional approaches to repair the damage. It was stories that distracted and got the message through.

Allow the audience to "discover" the message. The message is not coming as an assertion but is embedded in the story to be discovered by the audience or it is motivated by the story and thus more accepted. We know from research and common sense that self-discovery is much more powerful than having people talk at you. There is no person trying to persuade, only a storyteller.

Engender liking and respect. A likable character, plot or setting can be transferred to the signature social program and its sponsoring firm. Psychologists call that process affect transfer and have shown it to exist in a host of studies. Signature stories that show the competence of operations or the impact on clients can be a vehicle to provide visibility, respect and admiration for the signature program or its supporting business brand.

Enhance loyalty by deepening the relationship with committed stakeholders. Think about any important relationship you might have. It will almost certainly contain background stories about the other person that allow you to understand him or her. They help you know what lies behind many of that person's values, opinions, and behaviors and might also provide emotional insight, which is the basis of intimacy. By gaining a level of closeness based on a set of stories, the customer connection with your market niche and exemplar brand will be richer and more difficult to disrupt than if it were merely transactional. Stories add texture, substance and connection.

Multiple Story Sets

Often a single signature story is not adequate. It does not cover the scope and nuances of the signature social program. Further, a single story, even a powerful one, can quickly lose its novelty and its ability to stimulate retelling activity. So, in many cases, sets of signature stories are needed to provide more perspectives on the signature program and the opportunity to create freshness. The second and third Lifebuoy videos presented fresh stories with different heroes, contexts and experiences.

Multiple stories can elaborate and extend the message scope into different perspectives and contexts. Natalie was one of many charity: water stories each of which had a different perspective. Another story, for example, was about a person that spent his time repairing wells. The three KIND stories provide texture and depth to the "act of kindness" value of the organization. And Steve Rich was one of several Digital Eagle stories and they were part of a larger story set around Barclays' societal effort.

Each of the Dove stories from Chapter 2 was very different and yet provided a theme that helped the Real Beauty programs. Recall the early billboards with "Fat or Fab" question, stories about how make-up and digital alteration was used to "create" beauty, and that a women's self-description was much less flattering than that of an objective observer. Still another story found that many women faced with two side by side doors would enter the one marked "Average" instead of the one "Beautiful." The stories illustrate the fact that some 96% of women would not describe themselves as beautiful more vividly than just putting the fact on the table. The stories provide freshness, texture, and richness to the message.

Prophet has a monthly newsletter in which stories provide brand energy and support internally. A main vehicle are stories that reflect how the brand pillars and organizational values come to life in the form of employee initiatives and, customer experiences from the Prophet Impact set of programs. The flow of stories keeps the newsletter and its message relevant and inspirational and the employees and teams appreciated and connected.

Barriers to Story Use

Given the power of stories and the importance of content, why aren't stories used more extensively to communicate strategic messaging? Three reasons stand out and represent challenges that need to be overcome:

Gaining commitment to stories. Many people, especially in the social program world, think that communicating facts with clarity and punch is more efficient than telling a story, with its indirect and partial message. When communicating a set of points is the goal, there may be no currently available story that works for all elements to be communicated.

This straight-forward, fact-led strategy is supported by an assumption that audiences are always rational, motivated, and able to find and process objective information based in part on a belief that the information will be perceived as interesting and useful. This comfortable assumption, of course, rarely holds. Audience biases are particularly in evidence when the information is not of sufficient interest to gain attention or when prior beliefs lead them to filter or distort information that is inconsistent with what they "know."

There needs to be an organizational commitment to the need for stories to create attention, deflect counterarguing and other coping mechanisms, and to introduce emotion and empathy into the conversation. However, this is not enough. Two more tasks remain.

Finding great signature stories—those that attract attention, create interest, and avoid counter-arguing is difficult. It is usually not enough to wait for stories to surface. There needs to be a process to seek them out. Just having a person or team sniffing around for a hint of a compelling story with the capability of considering how it would be presented and leveraged can uncover stories. If you don't look, you are unlikely to find. And if there exists a "go to" person or team, it is more likely that a compelling story idea would become visible.

Stories can come from different sources. Recipients or clients of a signature social program are often rich targets because of the emotional impact of their stories and the fact that they are real people that the audience can get to know. The fear that they will be reluctant to share is usually misplaced and, in any case, the personal identities can be masked. Another source is the "heritage" story about the how and why of the signature program's beginning or of landmarks in its evolution. Another option would be a story around its program operations, including a difficult challenge and how it was overcome.

Incentivizing with a contest, another avenue, will automatically result in amazing stories, simply because of the numbers and the motivation of the story tellers. At the outset of the chapter there was the "My Story Storytelling Challenge," of HP in partnership with Girl Rising that attracted the personal stories of women around the world who recounted facing difficult challenges or intriguing situations. Other firms have employees compete with stories about their volunteer efforts. The core idea is to uncover well-hidden powerful stories. The contest itself will usually provide a communication opportunity about a firm's societal effort that will contribute to its visibility and credibility.

Presenting them effectively. Finally, the resulting story needs to be presented effectively to the target audiences. A great presentation cannot save a weak, placid story. However, a great story can be undercut by a weak presentation. That means creating professional presentations in print or video, using social video expertly, and developing an affordable media strategy. It is complicated by the fact that the relevant stakeholders can be diverse and not share media outlets. Resources for signature programs are limited but sometimes the profession talent can exist in the volunteer team and creative ways can be found to implement an affordable communication media strategy.

Stories can be used by a sponsoring firm or business that is an active partner and is motivated to connect to the signature program. The sponsoring firm will have communication assets, budgets, and media power to make a difference.

For more see my book Creating Signature Stories.[79]

We now turn to the "Must Do 4," the search for silver bullet brands.

Chapter 14

MUST-DO 4
FIND & FIRE YOUR
SILVER BULLET BRANDS

*The strength of the team is each individual member,
the strength of each member is the team.*

Phil Jackson, winner 11 NBA titles

Radical Hospitality

L ava Mae, the nonprofit that developed portable showers for the homeless, which will be discussed in the next chapter, had a philosophy that clients, mostly homeless, should be treated as friends. As such, Lava Mae staff and volunteers would never appear superior and condescending, but, rather, would ask them as a new friend about their background and interests. The goal is a relationship that is beyond functional. This attitude and behavior about client service was branded as "Radical Hospitality."

The brand made all the difference. It became a symbol internally and externally of the importance of keeping this policy front and center when delivering or communicating their service. It affected the expectation of those they served and, indeed, affected the experience itself. When the brand name was elicited, everyone in or close to Lava Mae knows exactly what that implied. It became an ongoing anchor to communicating and understanding internally and externally and the most important pillar of the brand vision, the most differentiating and resonating. It was their secret sauce. Think about it, a relationship style was branded. Think about what it did to not only the clients but all the stakeholders.

Such a brand is termed a silver bullet brand.[80] It is a branded feature, service, founder, story, or endorser or other "secret source" that provides energy, differentiation, or credibility to the signature social program. It can be provide an answer to the question—"Why this program?" If you ask why people are drawn to your brand, and the answer is not branded, you may have missed an opportunity. The signature social brand, the Dove Self-Esteem Program, for example, is enhanced by a set of silver bullet brands, Confident Me, Uniquely Me, and True to Me, all programs for teens. The silver bullet status elevates their priority within the social brand vision and communication effort.

Any social program, or any firm or organization for that matter, will have a team of brands. There are usually many of them. The challenge is to harness that team to create clarity instead of confusion, and to assign roles that enable a brand to help other brands. A silver bullet is one such role and plays an important part of a total brand portfolio strategy and in understanding and communicating the signature social program.

In this chapter, the challenge is to identity and prioritize potential silver bullet brands that can have a major role in enhancing the signature social programs. These brands can be part of the signature social programs or they can be external to it. The goal is to make sure that they are not undervalued or even taken for granted or ignored but, rather, resourced and actively managed.

Branded Differentiators, Energizers, & Sources of Credibility

All signature impact programs, like all brands, need differentiation, energy, and credibility. One route to gaining one or more of these three brand attributes is to create branded differentiators, branded energizers, and/or branded sources of credibility. All may be candidates to be silver bullet brands.

Differentiation, creating an ownable point of difference, matters. Both experience and research findings confirm this. There have been hundreds of studies, for example, exploring what makes new offerings successful. The single best predictor, by far, is how different the new offering is from what came before. This is partially because something new and different sparks interest by breaking through the clutter and information overload and, in part, because being different makes it likely that something worthwhile has appeared. Showing that it is contributing in a new and different way is helpful in getting buy-in and support from all the stakeholders. Demonstrating a real difference can also lead to energy and credibility.

For "Help a Child Reach 5," for example, the School of Five superhero brand plays a silver bullet role by demonstrating that the "Help a Child Reach 5" brand has developed its own style that will relate to the target audience. It does not attempt to force-feed school kids the facts and rules of hygiene.

Energy. All brands need energy—hustle and bustle with a sense of moving forward. A brand that lacks energy will lose momentum and relevance. It comes off as old-fashioned, conventional, out of touch, boring and not innovative. It may be reliable, honest, a hard worker and an excellent choice for your grandparents, but not you. A brand that loses energy gets relegated to the graveyard—where brands reside when even people that are familiar with the brand name fail to remember it.

The Dove Self Esteem program found energy in several silver bullet brands in addition to the teen programs. Confident Me, Uniquely Me, and True to Me. The global initiative, the "Free Being Me" self-confidence program, for example, became a potential silver bullet brand with the energy generated by fun and interactive activities to teach kids and young people the value of appreciating their own bodies.

Credibility. A signature social program, like any branded offering, needs credibility. There needs to be a feeling that the program organization has the resources, knowledge, and ability to actually operate the program and the commitment to see it through, when faced with barriers and difficulties. It needs reassurance in some tangible and substantive way. Some proof points are necessary. Without credibility, it is hard to have differentiation or energy that matters.

Think of how the Technology for Social Change provides credibility to the Salesforce commitment to provide at least 1% their product sales to societal good. In this case, an umbrella brand is also playing a silver bullet role.

Assuming multiple roles. A silver bullet can often take on several of these roles and sometimes all three. As noted in Chapter 12, Patagonia, the clothing firm with a mission to "save our home planet," has a signature social program, Worn Wear, that allows customers to return garments to be reused or recycled. Worn Wear has, in turn, a branded silver bullet, Worn Wear Recrafted, where the fabric from used clothing was used to make new garments which represented a creative and ambitious effort to reuse a brand that serves to differentiate, energize, and provide credibility, all three are activated.

The Real Beauty companion program provided a spark that provided a platform for Dove Self Esteem to enter on an energy high and a point of credibility as well. In that context, it played a silver bullet role as well as a signature program role. Similarly, the Nonprofit Cloud, the Education Cloud and the Philanthropy Cloud are all signature social programs that play a silver bullet role providing credibility to the Technology for Social Change brand.

A silver bullet study

The ability of a branded differentiator, energizer, or credibility source to enhance a brand was dramatically shown in a study of branded attributes. Carpenter, Glazer, and Nakamoto, three prominent academic researchers, found that the inclusion of a branded attribute (such as "Alpine Class" fill for a down jacket, "Authentic Milanese" for pasta, and "Studio Designed" for compact disc players) justified a higher price in the eyes of the respondents.[81] Remarkably, the effect occurred, even when the respondents were given information implying that the attribute was not relevant to their choice. Just the fact that there was a branded feature or component that signaled something special was enough.

The Silver Bullet Needs a Strong & Actively Managed Brand

A silver bullet brand needs to be strong and actively managed to perform its function of contributing energy, differentiation, and credibility to the signature social brand. Too often it is unbranded, described with pride to others but with no brand to help its role be communicated. In effect, it is hidden in plain sight. Or it could have a brand that has become a descriptor that is under appreciated internally and under communicated externally. Or the potential silver bullet brand may be a well-known, partner brand that is taken for granted, underleveraged, and needs an increase in status and a more visible link to the signature brand.

Recall some of what a brand does.

Just having a brand provides credibility both internally to employees and to external stakeholders. They all realize that a brand status implies a commitment and a willingness to stand behind its promises that affects perceptions and actions.

A brand and its symbols make it easier to communicate what the signature program does and to give it external and internal visibility. The silver bullet brand name, logo or tagline can be visually presented to remind and to connect to the social program. It provides a way to remind why the signature program is special.

A brand helps own the silver bullet content. Others may copy Radical Hospitality with a description of how they interact with clients, but they cannot deliver Radical Hospitality or even be a thought leader in that space because that brand is not available to them. Owning a silver bullet brand can better position a signature social brand to be the exemplar for its approach. It will also enhance stakeholder ability to articulate and commit to its purpose or mission.

Silver Bullet Brands within the Signature Programs

One source of silver bullet brands for a signature social program will be its branded programs or features. These will often have the potential to create energy, differentiation, and credibility for the program because they represent substance behind the promise. Recall the Barclays Digital Eagles that got people to thrive in the digital world using two silver bullet brands, the Tea and Teach in-bank earning session and the Digital Wings online courses.

It can be a process. For example, Shibusa provides a holistic approach to building homes that has advances in construction economics and the use of environmentally sensitive materials and designs that promotes healthier living and accessibility to affordable housing. It uses modular construction, or manufactured housing, using a branded silver bullet building process, the

"Precision Component On-site Assembly™" that delivers credibility and distinctiveness.

Susan G. Komen for a Cure, a signature program for several of their sponsors, consists in part of over a dozen sibling branded programs that provide an enhancement to the master social program brand. These include:

- Fund raiser brands, such as the Komen Race for the Cure, a now classic three-day effort and the More than Pink Walk series of family friend events, have achieved widespread visibility, involvement, and partner participation.
- Komen Scientific Research Grants with a peer reviewed process.
- Cancer patient services programs. The Komen's Metastatic Breast Cancer (MBC) Impact Series provides people living with metastatic breast cancer and their loved ones a safe, collaborative space to gather information related to MBC. Its Big Data for Breast Cancer (BD4BC) initiative where data is harvested to provide insights leading to treatments and care. The Treatment Assistance organization helps patients to cover the costs associated with treatments. Finally, the Patient Navigation Program helps patients navigate the complexities of the medical system and their illness.
- Programs directed at black women who are especially vulnerable, such as Komen's African-American Health Equity Initiative (AAHEI) that helps black women assess their risk and My Own Voice events, where black women living with MBC tell their story to help and inspire.
- Public policy programs such as The Susan G. Komen Center for Public Policy and the Komen Advocacy Summit.

The challenge is to set priorities. Which of these dozen or so brands, should be elevated to a silver bullet status? Which will make a difference for the Komen brand? Which will add differentiation, energy, or credibility?

It will clearly depend on the stakeholder audience. Each may play a silver bullet role in the particular context in which they are most relevant. The Race for a Cure can provide energy and differentiation to the Komen brand for employees, supporters, and families touched by cancer. The Komen Breast Care Helpline will provide credibility to affected families. Therefore, the resources devoted to the potential silver bullet brand and its link to the Komen master brand requires an analysis of the context, how important is it and how much the "silver bullet" role will help it. The challenge is to avoid understating the potential assistance that a silver bullet role can play in communicating the master signature social brand in various contexts and audiences.

Each of these sibling silver bullet brands for the Susan G. Komen for a Cure brand can also play a silver bullet role for each other. In that case, they will provide a depth of commitment, a willingness to expend substantial resources, and a serious understanding of the scope and complexity of the underlying social programs being addressed. There is a need to provide a link between the sibling brands as well as a link to the master social brand. Managing the brand portfolio becomes a crucial and challenging strategic task.

To brand or not to brand.

Whether to brand a feature of a signature social programs can be addressed by asking a few questions:

- Will it become a branded differentiator, energizer or credibility source that will have meaningful weight among some stakeholders? Is it a brand pillar or a key proof point of a brand pillar?
- Will it add clarity and efficiency to the internal or external communication task?
- If branded, will it be alive and serving a function in three to five years or will it fade?
- What is the cost of the needed brand building in not only money but added complexity?

The bottom line is that a "secret sauce" silver bullet brand is usually an opportunity that should not be overlooked.

Founder/CEO, Endorsers, and Partners as Silver Bullet Brands

Another source of silver bullet brands are founder or CEO brands, endorser brands, or external partner brands.

Founder/CEO brands.

The founder or CEO also has a personal brand that can sometimes help the signature social program gain differentiation, credibility and often energy as well. He or she might have a heritage story that can be important in motivating and explaining the purpose or mission.

Salesforce founder and CEO Marc Benioff, for example, provides energy, authenticity, and credibility to the Salesforce brand and its societal mission as well as the 1-1-1 (now Pledge 1%) program. His brand has been built by the heritage story of the 1-1-1 program, his very visible leadership in addressing societal challenges by not only by Salesforce but all firms, and his personal philanthropy. His funding, for example of the Marc Benioff Children's Hospitals, rubs off on Salesforce just as the Bill and Melinda Gates Foundation has helped the image of Microsoft. Paul Polman created a personal brand that played a similar role for Unilever, as did William Hesketh Lever over a century earlier for Lifebuoy that even today supports the "Help a Child Reach 5" program.

Endorser Brands

A social program out there by itself is often not credible. It will be perceived as lacking the resources or expertise to succeed. Having an endorsement from an organization such as Lifebuoy or Unilever that is substantial and successful can change the equation. It can install confidence that an endorsed social program brand will deliver on its promise, in part, because the endorser brand it is putting its reputation on the line. A key is to make sure that the endorser brands are linked to the signature social brand.

Internal endorsers. The endorsement can be within the organization containing the signature social program. It can be a business brand. The Lifebuoy brand, for example, endorses its "Help a Child Reach 5" signature programs. Endorsement of the program also can come from the corporate brand, Unilever, that will affect some stakeholders, such as employees, and suppliers.

In either case, the endorsement provides hard-to-earn credibility with its reassurance that an organization of substance stands behind the program, by putting its reputation on the line. The endorsement implies that an organization's visible resources, expertise and professional management skills will be available to the social programs.

A social program with a strong internal endorser will have the wind at its back and will be perceived as likely to succeed. The social program's ability to hire and communicate will become easier and success will be more probable than if the social program lacked visible endorsers. Think, for example, of making the "Help a Child Reach 5" program successful without the endorsement of Lifebuoy and the credibility that provides.

External endorsers. A firm with an ongoing effort to benefit a social program becomes a program endorser. Ford Motor Company, for example, active in the fight against breast cancer since 1993, started the Ford Warriors in Pink with a website with tips, tools and resources for cancer patients and survivors. The effort annually highlights 20 individual Models of Courage who have an inspiring breast cancer experience. One of the Warriors in Pink programs is to sell uniquely designed clothing items. All of the net proceeds are given to one of two charities, the Susan G. Komen for the Cure or the Pink Fund which provides financial support to meet the basic needs of cancer patients. In three decades, over 130 million dollars has been raised.

Ford through the Warriors in Pink program provides a visible endorsement of Komen and the Pink Fund. Ford could have picked any number of nonprofits to support but they picked Komen and the Pink Fund. People will correctly assume that the selection by Ford of these two nonprofits was made after considerable research on the effectiveness of relevant nonprofits. The willingness of Ford to attach their name and reputation to Komen and the Pink Fund would reassure a donor, a volunteer, or a patient.

Cause Marketing

Cause marketing refers to a promotional campaign of a business where the proceeds will benefit a cause or nonprofit. A classic example is where a percentage of the purchase price or profits would go to a nonprofit. The firm and its customers get to fund a nonprofit and enjoy the resulting self-expressive benefits. The nonprofit gets a visible promotional program that will enhance its brand awareness, a worthwhile stream of funding at no cost, and an endorsement of a prominent firm. The Ford Warriors in Pink programs that gave the proceeds of selling a line of uniquely designed clothing items to two charities is an example. What could go wrong?

It turns out that there are risks. There is the danger of developing a perception that the social appeal is only there to stimulate sales and make money especially if the sponsoring firm has a weak fit with the program. Another cause of skepticism is that the proceeds will be minimal or even nonexistent, despite the implied promise that the cash flow would be meaningful. In 2012, Komen had as many as 50 firms with promises to pay a portion of the proceeds to their charity. It turned out that some cosmetics products had cancer causing ingredients and a fast-food brand contributed to obesity, which is a cancer risk factor. Komen now screens for such risks.

To avoid or reduce these risks, the signature programs and the firm should make sure there is authenticity in the offer, the program has a long-term commitment, and a meaningful amount of money will go to the nonprofit. Ford's Warriors in Pink program, for example, was embedded in a long-term program, provided grants representing 100% of clothing purchases and, additionally, the items for sale did not involve a Ford vehicle.

Bank of America supports Komen through its Pink Ribbon Banking Affinity. There are "Pink Ribbon" credit cards and checking accounts, each of which earns money for Komen. Three elements of the program provide authenticity. First, using the Pink Ribbon logo provides a way for the customer to express their attachment to the Komen cause and to be part of a community. Second, it is part of a set of programs initiated in 2009 that includes being the National Presenting Sponsor of the Susan G. Komen 3-Day®, Race for the Cure® and More Than Pink Walk® events and having BofA employees volunteer for Komen. Third, they guarantee that at least $1.5 million per year will go to Komen from the affinity promise.

External Partner Silver Bullet Brands

An external partner brand can provide not only credibility but differentiation and energy. Dove's Self-Esteem Program alliance with the World Association of Girl Guides and Girl Scouts (WAGGGS) created the "Free Being Me" self-confidence programs reaching 4.5 million girls in five years. The Global Handwashing Day, started by Lifebuoy but with partners all over the world, reflects the uniqueness of the "Help a Child Reach 5" program and how it stands out among all the other societal efforts to combat water borne illness.

These partnership brands enhance the linked signature social programs. First, they vividly demonstrate that the social programs have scaled and that they are past the local stage. Second, it indicates that the firms are not interested in getting all the credit for the program by owning it. Instead, their goal is to impact and join with partners that will advance the goal. Third, the partner brands have a partner relationship with other respected brands. It is good company.

What is your "secret sauce"? What is it about your signature social program that makes it credible, differentiated, and have energy that is not as visible as it should be? Does it need a brand or does it need to have its brand made more prominent and be actively managed? Are there any external or internal brands that are part of the program that are underleveraged and could provide differentiation, energy, or credibility, if they were more prominent.

We next turn to the final imperative. If a signature social program works, scale it.

Chapter 15

MUST-DO 5
SCALE YOUR SIGNATURE
SOCIAL PROGRAM

"Thousands of candles can be lit from a single candle, and the life of the single candle will not be shortened. Happiness never decreases by being shared."
From Buddhist writings

T hink of an organization or nonprofit in your local community with a social program that really works. Across the world, hundreds of business firms and nonprofits have launched impactful, purpose-driven programs that are changing lives—but only in limited geographies and perhaps only in their local communities. Their mission, insight, and program details remain hidden from others wishing to address the same social problem or issue in other communities or geographies. Also, their role as a signature social program is limited to local sponsors.

If the purpose is to impact a societal need, it is eminently logical to scale it, to extend its reach to many more people by replicating it in other geographies or contexts. Breaking out of a local box has the potential to become more attractive to a national or global sponsor. It just makes sense. Yet social program leaders, whether in nonprofits or within a firm, have a lot on their plates and too often scaling is a back burner project or not considered at all.

Recall the Salesforce Pledge 1% (originally 1-1-1) program that provided a platform from which a robust societal effort has been liberated by the commitment of over 10,000 firms. By itself, it affected the Salesforce societal effort and became a brand pillar providing clarity about its commitment. When other firms accepted the challenge and made a similar commitment, the program went from being an influencer at Salesforce to being a game-changer for the whole national and global societal effort. Its impact was many orders of magnitude greater than when it was restricted to covering Salesforce. The effort involved explaining the program in talks and interviews often by Marc Benioff, by having the easy-to-understand descriptions on the website, and the intriguing and timely challenge. The effort involved little cost and by shining a light on the Salesforce societal efforts provided an immediate benefit.

Patagonia's 1% for the Planet pledge, discussed in chapter 12, that has attracted over 2,000 signatories, is another example. The passion and commitment of Patagonia for environmental action provided the leadership and credibility that attracted other firms. Think about it, the branded program with a visible role model impacted 2,000 firms.

Recall also the success of Goldman's 10,000 Women program and how its core idea of providing management training and mentoring led to the 10,000 Small Business Program. The momentum of both programs stimulated the One Million Back Women initiative which had a broader focus but also a brand that reflected a quantitative, ambitious goal and included an educational and mentoring dimension. It is unlikely that the last two programs would have happened without their ability to scale the ideas and outcomes of the first.

Lifebuoy's "Help a Child Reach 5" success in India led the program to be expanded to 28 countries. In doing so, it was sometimes adapted with innovations that were ultimately shared with other countries to enhance the program's impact.

Consider Lava Mae, a story of an inspiring role model on how to scale an idea.

Lava Mae—A Scaling Story

In 2013, San Franciscan Doniece Sandoval was inspired to take action after learning two heart wrenching stories: several of her elderly neighbors become homeless after being evicted from their homes following a huge rent increase and a homeless woman she met shared a fear of never being clean again. After learning that there were only 16 showers for 7,000 homeless people in the city, she resolved to find a way to provide showers to the homeless (she often calls them "unhoused").

A few months later, she proposed the concept of repurposing discarded Muni buses to provide showers and toilet services for these homeless. She got the busses, the know-how to convert them, and a staff. As a result, they were soon providing showers on the streets, which provided a step toward restoring dignity and rekindling optimism. She called her new organization Lava Mae (which means "wash me" in Spanish).

A key ingredient from the outset, introduced in the last chapter, was a branded relationship style or approach, "Radical Hospitality," a concept rooted in the basic principle—*how* you serve people is just as critical as the service itself. In Lava Mae words: "We're in the Hospitality business servicing guests. We build something beautiful for them to use, we know their names, and we learn their stories. We want them to feel better than when they arrived. It's the unexpected level of care that restores dignity; that rekindles hope and optimism and fuels the sense of opportunity vital to stopping the vicious cycle of homelessness."

A successful start in the Bay Area and Los Angeles resulted in each bus providing 2,000 showers each week. Experience and learning provided insights. The first insight—their guests lacked access to handwashing, a critical part of fighting sickness. In response, Lava Mae introduced handwashing stations, portable places where people could go and wash their hands the right way. Each station could handle 500 hand washing events before its daily refresh.

Another insight came from numerous stories about the difficulties the homeless face accessing critical services. They go from provider to provider, stand in long lines, and fill out duplicate information time and time again. And, maybe more important, their lack of positive social experiences, just having fun, was debilitating.

The response was the creation in 2016 of Pop-Up Care Villages, which are like a farmer's market of 20 or so real-time services. In addition to providing baseline needs for food (food trucks, bagged lunches, snacks, coffee), hygiene (showers, toilets, hygiene kits), and clothing (mending, laundry) there were health services (health screening, vaccinations, dental, vision) well-being (meditation, therapy, massage), employment opportunities, routes to housing, educational possibilities, and legal assistance. All this took place in a festive atmosphere with musicians decorations, games, and workshops that provided a party experience.

From the outset, Lava Mae gained visibility in part because of its positive press coverage. It attracted active sponsors, one of which was Unilever. The Lava Mae organization began to get numerous inquiries about how to establish services for the homeless in other communities. As a result, Lava Mae launched a "how to" guide and consultation service to enable others to duplicate its methods. By 2019, this effort was getting traction.

In 2020, Lava Mae decided to explicitly change its mission from providing local services to being an accelerator and support network for organizations throughout the world desiring to serve the homeless. Describing the new strategic thrust they noted that: "LavaMae^X is a nonprofit that teaches and funds organizations around the world to bring mobile showers and other services that promote well-being to people experiencing homelessness." The mission is "to change the way the world sees and serves our neighbors that are homeless."[82]

The new mission and a new name, LavaMae^X, was to provide 1:1 program consulting, free and fee-based in-depth training, do-it-yourself toolkits, a community, and ongoing support to help people and organizations around the world launch and sustain LavaMae^X-designed programs with the Radical Hospitality® approach.

The core of the new LavaMae^X strategic thrust are its programs to support those that aspire to start or want to improve a homeless service program bringing mobile showers and other care services to the streets. Toolkits were developed that covered topics like showers, handwashing stations, PopUp Care villages, and public relations. The PopUp Care toolkit for example, showed how to learn guest needs (with a guest advisory committee), find and recruit partners to match those needs, attract guest interest, transport guests, manage volunteers, provide a fun uplifting social experience, budget the event, plan a timeline, and get client feedback. It really is a "turn the crank" set of guides and instructions coordinated by the lavaMaex.org website.

An important addition was LavaMae^X Connect, a global community of people who are at all stages of bringing mobile showers and other care services to the street. Members get access to training events, do-it-yourself toolkits, community discussions, and troubleshooting support from LavaMae^X and from other members. It is a place where they can share best practice success stories, questions, challenges, information on governmental programs, and opinions. A participant receives not only practical ideas but also visibility and social support.

An interesting aspect of the LavaMae^X was how it attracts prospects all over the world. Some prospects already knew of Lava Mae because of the press attention that it had received over the years. It has always been an intriguing story. They simply called or visited the website. The rest were people that became interested in the problems of the homeless and found LavaMae^X on their own with a search engine using key words, such as homeless or portable showers. There was little active outreach seeking clients.

In less than two years, LavaMae^X mentored nearly 80 providers and birthed 14 new programs in 14 cities. In addition, over 7,500 kits were downloaded, many of which ultimately resulted in programs getting activated. In the meantime, a modest active service of providing showers, handwashing stations, and Pop-Up Care Villages in California remained in place, mainly as vehicles to train staff and to discover and test ideas for new or improved services

All of this was achieved from a simple idea formed just over eight years before. It was an idea built with a mission that gave it the wings to go from local to global. Imagine what your organization could achieve—and the lives it could change—with a program with the will to scale.

Right to Shower brand. Laura Fruitmant, then a new Unilever brand hire chatted with a NYC homeless man in NYC and was emotionally touched by learning that no one would talk to him. Years later, in September 2017, as a senior brand executive at Unilever and inspired by a TED talk by Doniece Sandoval, she pitched the idea of a branded soap and body wash line that would showcase what a shower meant to the homeless and allocate 30% of its profits to provide shower access via Lava Mae. Unilever, a Lava Mae partner, said yes.

Creating a new line and brand involved a lot of work. The product goal was to have natural ingredients, "no nasties," and still create lather. It was a substantial development challenge. Four fragrances were needed, one for each of four branded emotions that the brand wanted to create. The result: tangerine/honeysuckle for Joy; red ginger/current for Strength; aloe/dewy moss for Hope, and charcoal/cotton blossom signaled Dignity. Distribution began with Whole Foods, which was in keeping with its natural features and purpose-driven mission. The price was higher that mainstream products, in keeping with specialty soaps at Whole Foods and similar outlets.

The new line of soaps and body washes was introduced in 2019 under the brand name "Right to Shower." The brand name, by itself, tells the story of the product concept and calls attention to the condition of the homeless. Putting the purpose on the package as the brand name, was certainly a unique and powerful way to advance the cause. The Right to Shower business not only provided funding for LavaMae[X], but also provided a voice to amplify the Lava Mae mission and stories far beyond what otherwise would be possible. It is an example of what can emerge when a social program is integrated into a partner firm.

The Food Bank

John van Hengel was a retired businessman in Phoenix in 1967 and a volunteer at a soup kitchen. He was introduced to a mother of ten who fed her kids with food discarded by grocery stores and expressed a desire for a place where unwanted food could be collected and given to the hungry. Hengel verified that much of the dumpster food was edible and established the St. Mary's "food bank," financed by a loan of $3,000 from a church of that name. The St. Mary's food bank developed partnerships with grocery stores, food producers, and social welfare organizations throughout Phoenix and created a pool of volunteers. The need was there, and the St. Mary's food bank grew quickly, distributing over a million pounds of food by the second year.

Word of the food bank's success quickly spread and by 1977 food banks had been established in 18 cities across the country. With a solid base and considerable momentum, van Hengel, with help from a federal grant in 1979, created a national organization for food banks, Second Harvest. It changed its name in 2008 to Feeding America, far more descriptive and emotionally appealing. Fast forward to 2020, Feeding America is the nation's largest domestic, hunger-relief organization with over 200 food banks across the country providing an option for the 40 million people at risk of hunger, including 12 million children and 7 million seniors.

The headquarters of the Feeding America organization provides several services. It:

- Creates awareness about the extent of food insecurity and what that means to individuals based in part on its research about the extent and nature of the need for food support overall but also for segments, such as kids, teens, seniors.

- Lobbies the government for more support for the needy in the agricultural program and elsewhere.

- Supports the member food banks by sharing details about innovations and best-of-class programs and provides meetings and newsletters in which all the members can learn and interact.

- Provides a fund-raising vehicle for firms that are well-suited to partner with a national social program rather that local ones. The most committed become visionary partners.

- Offers ownable sponsorship niches. The Walmart Foundation, for example, underwrote the Feeding America effort to help low-income individuals connect to the SNAP (Supplemental Nutrition Assistance Program) program that subsidizes food purchases.

All this is in place because a small local idea got scaled.

Ronald McDonald House

A social program may seem too modest and crude to be scaled. However, if the underlying need is visible and real, the program might evolve and become scalable. That was the case with Ronald McDonald's House. In 1972, three-year-old Kim Hill, daughter of a Philadelphia Eagles football player Fred Hill and his wife Fran, was treated for leukemia at a Philadelphia hospital for children.

During the three years of treatment, Fred and Fran camped out in chairs and benches and ate from vending machines with other parents, some of whom lived some distance away from the hospital and could not afford a hotel.

The head of the pediatric oncology hospital dreamed of a comfortable residence for the affected family members and had the support of the Eagles. The regional McDonald's manager together with the local McDonald's ad agency stepped in with a St. Patrick's Day Green Milkshake (now known as the Shamrock Shake) promotion, which raised money to buy an old house near the hospital, which became the first Ronald McDonald House.

The number of houses grew to 10 in 1979, 60 by 1984 and nearly 400 in 2020 operating in 65 countries. Over 10 million families have been housed since 1974. Several observations.

First, the initial effort was modest and virtually unnoticed. However, McDonald's had a supporting promotion that provided money as well as visibility. It then hit a nerve and grew quickly, becoming a signature social program for McDonald's.

Second, this effort had considerable empathetic energy. It reached kids and parents, which are an important part of the customer base. The promotion was relevant and meaningful to them.

Third, the program was extended to over 200 Ronald McDonald's Family Rooms that accommodate families that might not need to travel from their home but still need a safe place to rest, wash clothes etc., while being close to their child. In addition, by 2020 over 50 Ronald McDonald's Care Mobiles in nine countries that offer health care clinics for children in their own neighborhoods at no cost to the families were established.

Learnings on Scaling

These three stories plus the experience of Pledge 1%, 1% for the Planet, Goldmans 10,000 Women, and Lifebuoy's "Help a Child Reach 5" are by no means a random sample of programs that have scaled but are representative examples of successful scaling efforts and offer some learnings.

First, all started as modest efforts that were stimulated by a person or a team within a firm who observed a social need that seemed unconscionable particularly in a rich, enlightened country when a feasible solution was in sight. That person or team had the talent and energy to engineer the program, attract volunteers, find financial backing, put a test version onto the street, and entice sponsoring firms or businesses to get involved.

Second, the impact of a social program can be enhanced, by adding features and services. Lava Mae added Handwashing Stations and Pop-Up Care Villages, both of which expanded the impact in terms of services and people. These innovations naturally come from hands-on contact with clients and a commitment to "deep listening."

Third, the big payoff comes from expanding the footprint and going regional, national or global. The numbers then can get huge and along with them, the impact of the program.

Fourth, the cornerstone of scaling is to codify success, to be able to communicate to others that are motivated to start a program in their area. There are several levels and stages of help possible.

- Understand and explain what you do. What are the basic keys to success? What is the path to getting them right? What are the challenges and how do you deal with them?

- Develop a process to handle incoming request for help. Answer basic questions from interested people. Create formal information kits that outline the steps to take and how to make sure the program is working well.

- Develop dedicated consulting people or teams. Created training programs which can be remote or on tape. Encourage adaptation and innovation.

- Activate visibility programs with postings on social media, talks, podcasts, articles, media appearances, stories by providing or sharing content. Reach out to complementary programs.

- Create communities of leaders and participants of active and potential programs with its own website where experiences, questions, challenges, and resources can be shared with a community that provides support. They are not alone.

Scaling does not have to be extensive, expensive, or absorb a lot of resources. If an idea emerges that is good but small, it might be enough to spread the idea with reach-out talks, interviews, or podcasts. If a program is replicated or extended even a few times, the program impact will be multiplied. It does not have to involve 200 replications, each with a major budget. Even scaling a major program, like LavaMae[X] has done, does not have to involve an expensive communication budget or an extensive consulting staff. It is like the Field of Dreams movie about building a baseball diamond—"If you build it, they will come." "They" will find you, given your media attention and website.

Chapter 16

EVALUATING YOUR SIGNATURE SOCIAL PROGRAM & BRAND

It ain't over til it's over.

Yogi Berra, Former NY Yankee and Philosopher

How do you measure success of your signature program and its brand? There follows a dozen indicators that can be used to evaluate existing or proposed programs and to compare them with alternatives.

Social need resonates. The motivating need is visible and has gotten traction. People care, believe the need to be meaningful.

Credibility. The program is perceived to work. It has the endorsement of major respected people and organizations. The concept is logical, there is face validity, and the needed talent and resources to make it work are available. Its operation is proven in the field.

Impact. There was convincing evidence of program participation and its impact on the motivating societal need. There were experiments or tests and case studies in the field that demonstrated results.

Authenticity. The program flows from and supports the culture and values of the firm and is one of their symbols and key proof points. The firm is perceived to have real passion about the societal need exhibited by persistent communication, by expending resources, and by making a long-term commitment. There is little evidence of perceptions that the program is token, not serious, phony, or "selling."

Stories. The program precipitates signature stores that attract attention and are memorable because of their emotional content, humor, relevance, or informativeness.

Visibility and Clarity. The program is intriguing and attracts attention. It is known by the stakeholders that matter, they understand the basics of the program and know the key elements that make it unique and effective.

Buy-in. The relevant stakeholders have accepted, even endorsed, the program as worthwhile and as part of the firm's culture and values.

Engagement. A worthwhile portion of important stakeholders have engaged in the program by volunteering, donating, advising, or otherwise joining some part of the program. They are not only committed by engaging but also by being ambassadors for the program. There is an active brand community.

Enhances a business brand. It influences the visibility, the image, and the loyalty of the stakeholders of a business brand. This influence makes a difference in business performance.

The brand team. Each brand has a clear role. Opportunities for umbrella brands, silver bullet brands, organizational brands, and subbrands are not missed or mishandled.

Business partner's support. The support should be on-going and can be in the form of visible endorsement, grants, volunteers, or access to relevant nd useful assets.

Scaling. There is a strategy to extend the program into new geographies or segments or to broadened it so that it does more.

ACKNOWLEDGEMENTS

owe a huge debt to all those firms and nonprofits that have successfully addressed serious challenges facing society and made a difference. I have been impressed with their drive, innovation, willingness to put in effort, and shear competence. I have learned so much from their efforts, not only about how social impact is created but also why there is such passion to succeed. Truly uplifting in these times of struggle and pessimism.

Among those that I have had a chance to connect and work with are Larry Sly of the Food Bank of Contra Costa, Sandra Scherer of the Monument Crisis Center. Eve Birge of the White Pony Express, Doniece Sandoval of Lavamae[x,] Samir Singh of Lifebuoy, Andy Amstutz and Don Jenkins of the Village, and Richard Lyons of the BerkeleyHaas School of Business. There are others who have served as role models for many such as Marc Benioff of Salesforce, Paul Polman of Unilever, and Yvon Chouinard of Patagonia whose stories are recounted in this book. I applaud and thank them all for their leadership.

I also owe much gratitude to those many authors that over the decades have contributed to our knowledge and practice of dealing with social challenges. This book rests on the shoulders of many. It is a long list.

I need to thank my colleagues at Prophet, the branding and transformation consultancy with which I am associated. It is a pleasure to be among a group so talented, collegial, and ready to be involved in social issues and problems. I am especially appreciative of the support of Scott Davis whose instinct gets me to a better place. But many others helped as well when I needed them, people like John Ellet, Peter Dixon, Jay Millikan, Marisa Mulvihill, Ted Moser and many others. Mandy Stehouwer and Lazzarus Ciurliza made the figures interesting and clear. Stren Pipkin and Dani Kim, gifted designers and patient collaborators, created an assertive cover that, in my view, has pop, content, and intrigue. And the marketing team, Michelle Galliani, Kristen Moore, and Amanda Nizzere have elevated my voice with professional skill. All this is driven by my friend and exceptional CEO, Michael Dunn, who is over-the-top committed to tackle social problems. When they emerge with urgency, Michael is always there.

Others have supported as well including friends such as Andy Smith—always there to advise or reassure, Marty Brant—my long-term brand compadre, Joe Tripodi—endorsed virtually all my books always with thoughtful and inspiring words, and Phil Kotler—my role model.

I am now on my fourth book with my partners at Morgan James Publishing, who replace stress in the process with confidence, creativity, and fun. David Hancock, its founder and CEO, is knowledgeable, insightful, positive, and supportive, and has been such a pleasure to work with. Jim Howard, its publisher, added helpful advice at crucial times. My brilliant copy editor, Lynsey Peyton elevated the book for sure and Emily Madison guided the book through the production process, never an easy task.

Finally, I would like to thank my family, my wife Kay and our daughters Jennifer, Jan and Jolyn who support and inspire me. They enrich my life in many ways. A special callout to Jennifer who strives to keep me rigorous, on brand and on topic, and has contributed substantively to virtually all of my work.

About the Author

David Aaker, the Vice-Chairman of Prophet (a global consultancy around branding, growth, and strategic transformation) and Professor Emeritus of Marketing Strategy at the Berkeley-Haas School of Business, is the winner of five career awards for contributions to the science of the theory and practice of marketing including the MIT's Buck Weaver Award and the NYAMA Marketing Hall of Fame. He has published more than one hundred articles and eighteen books that have sold well over one million copies and been translated into eighteen languages. They include *Managing Brand Equity, Building Strong Brands, Brand Leadership* (co-authored with Erich Joachimsthaler) *Brand Portfolio Strategy, From Fargo to the World of Brands, 3rd edition, Spanning Silos, Strategic Market Management 11th edition, Brand Relevance: Making Competitors Irrelevant* which was named to three best book lists for 2011, *Aaker on Branding, Creating Signature Stories,* and *Owning Game-Changing Subcategories.* Named as one of the top five most important marketing/business gurus in 2007, Professor Aaker has won awards for the best article in the California Management Review and (twice) in the Journal of Marketing. A recognized authority on brand strategy, he has been an active consultant and speaker throughout the world. he regularly blogs at davidaaker.com and Linkedin and is at twitter.com/davidaaker. An avid biker and struggling golfer, he lives in Orinda California.

Endnotes

1   The Economist August 9, 2018, pp. 55-56.

2   Unilever Annual Report 2020, p. 11.

3   Unilever Annual report 2011; Globescan.com, 2011 Sustainability Leadership Report.

4   Unilever's CEO Has a Green Thumb, Fortune June 10, 2013 pp. 124-128.

5   Ibid.

6   unilever.com/sustainable-living/ourapproach/messageceo.

7   Unilever Annual Report, 2011.

8   Globescan.com/uilever-patagonia-idea-sustainabiltiy-leadershp-2019

9   Source: Unilever Annual Report 2020.

10   Alan Jope, CEO letter in the 2020 Unilever Annual Report.

11   Ibid.

12   Ibid.

13   Olivia Zed, "How Dove Real Beauty Campaign Won and Almost Lost Its Audience," RRweekApril 16, 2019

14   Dove.com 2022.

15   Mark Kramer, Myriam Sidibe, and Gunjan Veda, "Dove and Real Beauty: Building a Brand with Purpose," Case 9-720-361, Harvard Bueinss School, June 14, 2021. p. 12.

16   Myriam Sidibe, Brand on a Mission, New York, NY Routledge, 2020, Chapter 2, p. 36.

17   Nicola Kemp, "Case Study: How AXE Redefined Masculinity," Campaingnlive.co.uk, April 10, 2017.

18   The descriptions of the Lifebuoy "Help a Child Reach 5" are sourced in part from Unilever.com, Lifebuoy Way of Life Special Mission Report 2019, July 2019.

19   Myriam Sidible, Brands on a Mission, NYC, Routlege, 2020, p. 7.

20   Myriam Sidibe, Marketing Meets Mission, Harvard Business Review, May-June, 2020.

21   Kanter Brand Footprint Report—2020, Kantar.com, July 2020.

22   Liky Kunda, "Ben & Jerry's, Black Lives Matter, and the Politics of Public Statement," Flowjournal.org/2020/07, 2020.

23   Unilever Sustainable Living Plan, 2010 to 2020, March, 2021, Assets. Unilever.com.

24   The material for the Salesforce story is taken in part from the book by the founder—Marc Benioff, Behind the Cloud, San Francisco: Jossey Bass, 2009 and the Website Salesforce.org, December, 2020. Material is also sourced from the Salesforce.org Social Impact Report, 2019 and the Salesforce Stakeholder Report of Fiscal Year 2022.

25   Dan Pontefract, "Salesforce CEO Marc Benioff Says The Business of Business Is Improving the State of the World," Forbes.com Jan 7 2017.

26   Jessica Raymond, "Five Life Lessons from Marc Benioff," news.USC. edu, Autumn, 2014.

27   Salesforce.org Social Impact Report 2019, pp. 1-2.

28   Salesforce Stakeholder Impact Report, 2020, p. 35.

29   Isabel Kelly, Foundation trip to St. Marints school, Kenya, Salesforce. org, May 4 2011.

30   Salesforce Stakeholder Impact Report, 2020.

31   Peter Drucker, The Practice of Management, Harper Perennial Publications, New Your, 1954.

32   "90% of S&P 500 Index Companies Publish Sustainability Reports in 2019, G&A Announces in its Latest Annual 2020 Flash Report." Globalnewswire.com, August 2021.

33   "The KPMG Survey of Sustainability Reporting 2020," home.kpmg.com, August 2021.

34   "A Leader's Guide: Finding and Keeping Your Next Chief Diversity Officer," RussellRenolds.com,

35   Michael Jensen,.& William Meckling, "Theory of the Firm: Managerial Behavior, Agency Costs and Ownership Structure." *Journal of Financial Economics*, 3, 1976, pp. 305-360.

36   David Gelles, "The Man Who Broke Capitalism," New York: Simon & Shuster, 2022.

37   IRS data.

38   Gelles, op. cit. p. 11.

39   Gelles, op. cit. Chapter 4.

40   "Business Roundtable Redefines the Purpose of a Corporation to Promote 'An Economy That Serves All Americans'" Business Round Table. org, AUG 19, 2019.

41   Alan Murray, "America's CEOs seek a New Purpose for the Corporation," Fortune, August 10 ,2019.

42   "Winning the Race to Net Zero: The CEO Guide to Climate Advantage," BCG & the World Economic Forum, January, 2021.

43   Jenny Gross, The Business School E.S.G. Boom, The New York Times, nytimes.com, November 13, 2021.

44   Robert G. Eccles and Svetlana Klimenko, The Investor Revolution, Harvard Business Review, May-June 2019 pp. 106-116.

45   Porter Novelli, Purpose Message Develops Greater Attention, Arousal, and Emotion, Conecomm.com, 2021Results summarized in Deloitte's 2020 Global Marketing Trends, deloitte.com, November 2021

46   "Winning the Race to Net Zero: The CEO Guide to Climate Advantage," BCG & the Wrold Economic Forum, January, 2021.

47   2016-millennial-employee-engagement-study, conecomm.com, November 2021.

48   Porter Novelli, Purpose Message Develops Greater Attention, Arousal, and Emotion, Conecomm.com, 2021

49   2020 Edelman Trust Barometer, Edelman,com, November, 2021.

50   "Environmental concerns and global citizenship: 2 worldviews shaping the way consumers shop," Advertising.Amazon.com 2021.

51   un.org/en/climatechange/reports

52   Thegiin.org.

53   GIIN's 2020 Annual Impact Investor, Thegiin.org.

54   Rachel Carson, "Silent Spring," New York: Houghton-Mifflen, 1962; Ralph Nader, Unsafe at Any Speed," Richard Grossman, New York, 1965; Betty Friedan, "The Feminine Mystic," W.W. Norton, New York, 1963.

55   The Climate Change Report 202,un.org/en/climatechange/reports, 2021.

56   "The Marketeer's ToolBox—Global Treads," WARC, Warc.com, January 2022.

57   Bill Gates, Annual Letter 2020, "Why We Swing For the Fences," Bill and Melinda Gates Foundation, GatesNotes.com

58   Edward O'Donnell, America in the Gilded Age and Progressive Era, Great Courses, 2015

59   "Unilever's purpose-led brands outperform," October 6, 2019 in Unilever.com, 2022.

60   Boris Groysberg, Jeremiah Lee, Jesse Price, and J. Yo-Jud Cheng, "The Leaders's Guide to Corporate Culture," Harvard Business Review, January-February, 2018. A few of the labels have been changed to make them more descriptive.

61   Personal communication from John Gerzema who noted that in 2008 Walmart was ranked number 12 on the social responsibility scale among 3,000 brands tracked by the Young & Rubicam's BrandAsset Valuator database.

62   Andrew S. Ross, "Green Project Making It Harder to Hate Walmart," San Francisco Chronicle, February 28, 2010.

63   EBD Staff, "100 Best ESG Companies: Top Stocks For Environmental, Social And Governance Values", Investors.com/news, January, 2022.

64   Myriam Sidibe, Brand On a Mission, New York: Routledge, 2020, pp. 13-16.

65   Sidibe, op. cit. p. 130

66   The PepsiCo story is documented in the PepsiCo Sustainability Report 2020.

67   Tom Roach, "Barclays: Purpose Pays," WARC, 2016.

68   Roach, op.cit.

69   John Elkington, "Towards the Sustainable Corporation: Win-Win-Win

Business Strategies for Sustainable Development," California Management Review, January, 1994, pp. 90-100.

70 2021 Edelman Trust Barometer, Edelman.com, November, 2021

71 David Aaker & Robert Jacobson, "The financial Information Content of Perceived Quality," Journal of Marketing Research, May, 1994, 191-201; David Aaker & Robert Jacobson, "The Value Relevance of Brand Attitude in High-Technology Markets," Journal of Marketing Research, November, 2001, 485-293.

72 Claes Fornell, Sunil Mithas, Forrest V. Morgeson III, & M.S. Krishnan, "Customer Satisfaction and Stock Prices: High Returns, Low Risk," Journal of Marketing, Jan 2006 pp. 1-14.

73 Interbrand Best Global Brands—2020 Learn.Interbrand.com, February, 2021.

74 Alex Edmans, Grow the Pie, Cambridge, UK, Cambridge University Press, 2020 pp. 78-85

75 Edmans, op cit p. 95.

76 David Aaker, Spanning Silos, Cambridge, Mass: Harvard Business Press, 2008.

77 Teachforamerica.org, 2022.

78 David Aaker, Creating Signature Stories, New York: MorganJames, 2018. Chapter 4.

79 Aaker, Op. Cit.

80 The Silver Bullet metaphor can be traced back to centuries old stories of how a silver bullet could bring down seemingly invulnerable nasty characters. The Lone Ranger, a masked man featured in twentieth century movies who fought for good (always successfully) in the old West, left a silver bullet behind as a symbol of how justice could overcome evil. The term can now be used as a metaphor for a simple, seemingly magical, solution to a complex problem.

81 Gregory Carpenter, Rashi Glazer, and Kent Nakamoto, "Meaningful brand Form Meaningless Differentiation: The Dependence on Irrelevant Attributes, Journal of Marketing Research, August, 1994, pp. 339-350.

82 LavaMae[x] Annual Report, Fiscal Year 2021.

Index

A free ebook edition is available with the purchase of this book.

To claim your free ebook edition:

1. Visit MorganJamesBOGO.com
2. Sign your name CLEARLY in the space
3. Complete the form and submit a photo of the entire copyright page
4. You or your friend can download the ebook to your preferred device

Morgan James
BOGO™

A **FREE** ebook edition is available for you or a friend with the purchase of this print book.

CLEARLY SIGN YOUR NAME ABOVE

Instructions to claim your free ebook edition:
1. Visit MorganJamesBOGO.com
2. Sign your name CLEARLY in the space above
3. Complete the form and submit a photo of this entire page
4. You or your friend can download the ebook to your preferred device

Print & Digital Together Forever.

Snap a photo

Free ebook

Read anywhere

Printed in the USA
CPSIA information can be obtained
at www.ICGtesting.com
JSHW022220140824
68134JS00018B/1170